Hugo's Language Books

This edition published in Great Britain
in 1997 by Hugo's Language Books,
an imprint of Dorling Kindersley Limited,
9 Henrietta Street, London WC2E 8PS

Visit us on the World Wide Web at http://www.dk.com

A CIP catalogue record is available from the British Library.

ISBN: 0 85285 297 5

'Hindi in Three Months' is also available in a pack with two
audio cassettes, ISBN: 0 85285 298 3

Written by **Mark Allerton**

Set in 10/12pt Palatino by **Alastair Wardle**

Reproduced, printed and bound in Italy by
L.E.G.O., Vicenza.

Contents

Introduction

This book is for travellers who want to be able to talk to the people they meet in India in the local language – even if such conversations are conducted on only a very basic level. It is designed to cover many of the dialogues that are likely to take place between an Indian and a foreigner, in probable situations such as in a shop or on a train. A foreigner in India will invariably be asked, either in Hindi or English, the same handful of introductory questions "Where are you from?", "Are you married?" and so forth. So, by learning these and their variations, you can gain an excellent foothold in Hindi and thereby build up the confidence you need to say more.

To learn gramatically correct Hindi, and to speak it fluently, is an immense task which this book will not attempt to address. However, to be able to chat to people is not so difficult, and it is hugely rewarding. Indian people who have never spoken to a foreigner before are often very eager to do so, even if they don't have a word of English. With a bit of Hindi, and the correct attitude, you can go right off the tourist track to villages where you will encounter the famous hospitality of the 'real' India. Here, the people are interested in you rather than your money (as is often the case in the cities). Without any doubt, if you can speak just a little Hindi, it will improve your time in India out of all proportion to the effort required in learning.

Hindi is the link language of most of India, being spoken as a first or second tongue by virtually all of Northern India, from Goa up to Kashmir, and across to Calcutta. As the 'official' language of around 700 million people, it ranks third in the world (after English and Chinese), although many of that number would not claim to be fluent in it. Mother-tongue speakers number some 200 million.

Hindi in Three Months is divided into two parts: the first consists of a simple guide to elements of the everyday spoken language, together with informative notes, which will give you enough to get by on; while the second is a more detailed grammar section, which provides extra tuition if you feel like it.

How to use this book

Adults acquiring a foreign language usually spend too long learning things theoretically and not long enough on the repetition of speaking and listening exercises, which is the only way to be able to hear and speak fast enough. It is vital, right from the outset, to learn to say phrases so fast that you can spit them out without consciously thinking about them. All languages are spoken extremely quickly: it is only because you can understand English that it doesn't seem fast. We are not suggesting you should learn loads of phrases, parrot-fashion; you need to know what it is that you're saying, and to translate the probable reply. The speedy delivery isn't meant to impress your listeners, but it should help them to understand what they hear. If you speak very slowly, albeit 'correctly' in terms of sentence construction and so forth, they are less likely to cut through your accent and grasp your meaning.

To speak simple and effective Hindi quickly, you need to learn a small number of key phrases fluently. To do this you should follow the three separate stages given below, in each chapter:

- Read each dialogue aloud, to see how the language 'works'.

- Repeat the phrases again and again, as fast as possible, to achieve a natural sound, and to be able to understand the words when they are spoken at a natural speed.

- Learn how to use each key phrase to make your own
  sentences. To do this, you must work very hard at all
  the exercises in the book. These are generally role-plays
  between an Indian and a foreign tourist. At this stage it is
  essential to use your imagination – to pretend that you
  are actually speaking in a real situation, and not just
  reciting strange Hindi words. If possible, do these
  exercises with a partner; if not, imagine that you have
  one. If you have the tape, listen to it over and over again,
  and repeat each phrase in the pause that follows. When
  you can do this easily, try to repeat it at least twice.

As soon as you feel that you have mastered a chapter –
which means that you can say the phrases without having
to think – you should try out what you have learnt. If you
are already in India, visit a Hindi-speaking shop-owner
and use your newly acquired phrases without lapsing into
English. Nothing will improve your confidence more than
actually placing a real live order for something to eat and
drink in a tea shop. Do it politely, confidently, and watch
the shopkeeper's surprised and impressed face as he or she
serves you. If possible, choose a small, quiet shop where
foreign tourists don't go and where English isn't spoken.
(Indian people who do know English will usually insist
upon using it.) Of course, if you're not yet in India you
might have to resort to your nearest Indian restaurant or
shop, but check first that the staff speak Hindi rather than
Gujarati, Punjabi or Bengali.

So, don't try to learn too much, too fast. Learn Chapter 1
thoroughly before moving on to Chapter 2. In this way, you
should be able to communicate well in Hindi from the very
start, and will have the confidence and motivation to go on.
A purist might say that you aren't speaking perfect – or
academically correct – Hindi, but as long as you can express
yourself and understand most of what is said to you, does
that really matter?

What about the grammar?

In Hindi, all nouns are masculine or feminine (with no logic to decide which). They can be singular, plural, honorific or 'oblique', and their endings change accordingly. Similar changes apply also to adjectives and verbs. In commonly spoken Hindi, though, such rules are blatantly disregarded, and all nouns (apart from a few obvious ones) are considered to be masculine singular. That is how people speak, and the dialogues in *Hindi in Three Months* are written in this informal style. It is a lot easier to learn, of course, but it can be technically incorrect; if you want to learn a little of the formal language, refer to the guide to essential 'hard' grammar towards the end of the book.

Formal Hindi is heard on news broadcasts and is spoken by a tiny minority of richer, well-educated Indians; in self-study courses based entirely upon the academic language and written by such people, you may find numerous polite expressions which you'll never hear spoken. For example, the man in the street won't say the Hindi equivalent of "Very pleased to meet you", but rather "Alright, brother". Learning formal Hindi will put you in a Catch 22 situation: you won't be able to use it to talk to well-educated Indians, because they speak very good English and insist on using it; but nor will you be able to speak to the other 90 per cent of the population, who use only 'common' Hindi.

Hindi in Three Months is designed to be as user-friendly as possible. It sacrifices 'perfect' grammar in order to make the language easier to learn. By cutting corners on grammar (as many Indians do), and by not attempting to achieve perfect pronunciation, you'll find that Hindi becomes much easier to speak.

Good luck !

Pronunciation

The pronunciation guide provided for words listed in each chapter, which gives a similar sounding or rhyming English word, is a simplified approximation of the Hindi sounds, and an easy way to remember the words. It should not be taken as exact. There's a round-up of the essential principles of Hindi pronunciation on the next few pages, but don't get too bogged down in them. To achieve good pronunciation in a foreign language you must try to imitate the sound of a native speaker. It isn't easy to say the sounds perfectly, but so long as they are more or less correct, and spoken fast and confidently, you should have no problem speaking Hindi.

If you have the two tapes, listen to the relevant track and try to sound exactly the same as the speakers: copy the rhythm, stress and intonation – as well as the pronunciation. The guide below describes how to make the sounds in Hindi so that you should be able to pronounce any words not heard on the recording.

Read through these pages to familiarise yourself with the basics of Hindi pronunciation, but don't attempt to 'learn' everything at this stage. Move quickly on to the next chapter, and refer back to these notes from time to time, when you feel the need to do so.

The Hindi words in this book have been transcribed by using a phonetic system which contains double vowels and capital letters in the middle of a word. This is because there are more sounds in Hindi than in English, and we have to differentiate between them. To avoid confusion (and because capital letters do not exist in Hindi script), the transcribed sentences start with a small letter unless a place-name is involved. To use this system you must learn a few rules, but remember that it is neither easy nor essential to pronounce Hindi letters perfectly, especially the consonants.

So, read this chapter, listen for the sounds on the tape, and copy what you hear. If you don't have the tape, interpret the imitation given in the book as best you can. In each chapter, words appear with their pronunciation given alongside in 'sound-alike' English words ("... sounds like 'racer'", "...like 'lay+kin'", "...rhymes with 'cart'", and so on). However hard you find it, remember that if you speak fast and with the correct rhythm, you'll be understood even if some of the letters are pronounced wrongly. If you pronounce the letters well but speak slowly and without confidence, you won't be understood. Luckily, in Hindi the vital letters aren't difficult and the difficult letters aren't vital.

Vowels

These are vital. As in English, if you confuse 'bit, bet, boat, bait', etc, no communication is possible. In Hindi there are five short and five long vowels.

Vowel	Hindi example	English example
a (short)	garam, bas, ham	above
aa (long)	aatii, baat, aap, khaalii	between 'cart' and 'cat'
i (short)	kitna, ki	it, sit, in, pin
ii (long)	jii, THiik, aatii, kii	seen, team
u (short)	kuchh, bahut	book, look, butch
uu (long)	ghuumna	boot, loot
e (short)	dena, ek, se	fed, egg
ai (long)	kaise, hai	fade, aid
o (short)	do, thoRa	so, low, go
au (long)	aur	plough, wow!

- All the above sounds exist in English, so there is no problem in saying them.

- The most important letter to get right is 'a'. This, in the middle of a word, is silent. Look at the English word 'banana'; here, the first 'a' is silent and the second 'a' is long. These two match 'a' and 'aa' in this book.

11

- There's not much difference between 'i' and 'ii', or 'e' and 'ai', so don't worry about these.

- 'u' and 'uu', and 'o' and 'au', are different but easy.

To make the pronunciation easier, in this book we have put a long 'aa' at the end of a word as if it was a short 'a'. In practice, however, you don't need to worry about vowels at the end of a word.

Nasalised vowels

In this book's transcription, nasalised vowels are written using small letters followed by a 'hash' mark (#): **haa#, nahii#**, etc. You must voice such vowels through your nose (which will wrinkle if you're doing it right). Practise these vowels repeatedly. There is no such sound in English, so it may feel strange at first. Other vowels are rarely nasalised.

Consonants

These are very difficult, so don't worry at all if you can't sound them correctly in the beginning. The worst thing to do is to speak slowly, in an attempt to perfect the pronunciation. Speak quickly, even if the result is incorrect.

- 'r' is much stronger than in English: rrroll it.

- 'w' is halfway between a 'v' and a 'w', but more like a 'w'.

- 'h' is spoken as in English if it comes first in a word: ham. If 'h' is in the middle of a word it is hardly sounded at all: **nahii#, rehna, mahanga**. As an exception to this rule, if the 'h' is in the middle and followed by a long 'aa', then it is spoken as in English: **kahaa#, rehaa**.

The other letters are arranged in a unique system to show how they should be pronounced:

A	B	C	D	E
kaa	kha	ga	gha	
cha	chha	ja	jha	
Ta	THa	Da	DHa	
ta	tha	da	dha	na
pa	pha	ba	bha	ma

Notice how columns B and D are the same as A and C but with an 'h' added. The sounds in B and D do not exist in English, so they are difficult; they are made by saying the letter with a lot of air coming out of the mouth (whereas no air is expelled with the sounds in A and C). Listen very carefully to the cassette. The difference between 'ba' and 'bha', and between 'kaa' and 'kha', is this air. You must realise by now that they represent completely different letters: for example, **kaali** means *black* while **khaali** means *empty.*

Practise by saying the alphabet with a piece of paper over your mouth. It should be still for columns A and C, and move for B and D. Also, to pronounce (for example) **gha** correctly, say 'hag-hag-hag' very quickly until the 'g' and 'h' combine.

These sounds will feel unnatural at first, but they aren't too difficult so long as you realise that they are different.

Look again at the same table. This time the lines have been numbered, to indicate whereabouts in the mouth they are sounded; see page 14 for the explanation of how each sound can be created.

	A	B	C	D	E
1.	kaa	kha	ga	gha	
2.	cha	chha	ja	jha	
3.	Ta	THa	Da	DHa	[*Ra RHa]
4.	ta	tha	da	dha	na
5.	pa	pha	ba	bha	ma

Line 1: from deep in the throat, with no lip or tongue movement.
Line 2: from the middle of the tongue.
Line 3: with the tongue pointing vertically upwards and touching the roof of the mouth strongly.
Line 4: with the tongue touching the edge of the upper front teeth, and just popping out of the mouth.
Line 5: with the lips touching each other.

Lines 1, 2 and 5 are straightforward. Lines 3 and 4 are very difficult because they represent two kinds of 't'; and an English 't' is spoken with the tongue touching the upper gums i.e. unlike either 3 or 4! If you want, you can simply ignore the difference between 3 and 4 and probably still be understood. But if you listen repeatedly to the tape you'll notice that letters in line 3 sound dull whereas those in line 4 sound crisp. If you watch someone speaking, you'll see the tongue when he or she pronounces line 4 letters.

Note that Indians consider that an English 't' sounds more like a 'Ta', not 'ta'. So, loan-words from English will be written **TikaT** *(ticket)*, **lanDan** *(London)*.

[*] 'Ra' and 'RHa' are variations of 'Da' and 'DHa'. To say them, you put your tongue in the vertical position, then flap it forward to make a strange sound somewhere between an 'r' and a 'd'. 'RHa' is an aspirated 'Ra'. If you want, just say 'Ra' like 'Da' and 'RHa' like 'DHa', this will be understood. But you must not say 'Ra' like '**ra**' because they are completely different.

Do not expect to be able to hear or say all these sounds correctly for ages; in time, your ear will pick them out and your tongue will get around them. Concentrate instead on learning lots of Hindi words and phrases.

The letters 'y', 'r', 'l', 'v', 'sh', 's' and 'h' do not fit into the above tables. They are all pronounced the same as in English, except that 'r' is much stronger and 'h' is almost silent in the middle of a word.

Reading Hindi script

The chief purpose of the tables below is to familiarise you
with the form of Hindi letters – but you may also be able
to use them to decipher whole words. (Learning to read
Hindi is more straightforward than most people think.)
Hindi words are formed by joining letters together with
a horizontal line.

Consonants

The consonants below are laid out as in the tables on page 13;
those that do not fit into the system are listed separately below.

A	B	C	D	E
kaa	kha	ga	gha	
क	ख	ग	घ	
cha	chha	ja	jha	
च	छ	ज	झ	
Ta	THa	Da	DHa	Ra/RHa
ट	ठ	ड	ढ	ड़ ढ़
ta	tha	da	dha	na
त	थ	द	ध	न
pa	pha	ba	bha	ma
प	फ	ब	भ	म

Notice that the difference between **dha** + **gha** and **bha** + **ma**
is the horizontal line on the top. Also notice that **Ra** is like
Da plus a dot. Consonants may be joined in a word by
removing the vertical bar from the first one.

y	r	l	v	s	sh	h
य	र	ल	व	स	श	ह

Vowels

Vowels have both a full written form and an abbreviated form. Fortunately, the latter is used 90 per cent of the time. The full version is used, for example, when a vowel begins a word or when one vowel follows another. Nasalised vowels are written by putting a dot over the letter.

Full form					*Abbreviated form*			
a	अ	aa	आ		a	*(none)*	aa	ा
i	इ	ii	ई		i	ि	ii	ी
u	उ	uu	ऊ		u	ु	uu	ू
e	ए	ai	ऐ		e	े	ai	ै
o	ओ	au	औ		o	ो	au	ौ

All abbreviated vowels are written after the consonants except 'i' (इ), which is written before, and u (ु) and uu (ू) are written under; and e (ए) and ai (ऐ) are written above. e.g:

कम	**kam**	less		स	**se**	from
काम	**kaam**	work		है	**hai**	is/are
कि	**ki**	or		दो	**do**	two
की	**kii**	of		सौ	**sao**	100
तुम	**tum**	you (familiar)				
तू	**tuu**	you (more familiar)				

Numbers

1	2	3	4	5	6	7	8	9	10
१	२	३	४	५	६	७	८	९	१०

Chapter 1

In the Tea Shop

In this chapter you'll learn how to ask for a drink and something to eat, the numbers 1–10, simple "what's this?" questions, and some general greetings. The dialogue includes all the most popular words in Hindi – **hay, haa#, nahii#, jii, THiik hay, achchhaa** – which form at least five per cent of any Hindi conversation that you're likely to have. Learn them fluently and you're well on the way to being understood.

Dialogue 1

Tea seller: **chaay, chaay, garam chaay!**
Tea, tea, hot tea!

Tourist: **anjii! chaay kitne paise hay?**
Hello. How much is tea?

Tea seller: **chaay ek rupeya hay.**
Tea is one rupee.

Tourist: **achchhaa? do chaay dena. yeh kyaa hay?**
I see. Two teas please. What's this?

Tea seller: **yeh samosa hay. yeh do rupeya hay.**
This is a samosa. It's two rupees.

Tourist: **achchhaa? THiik hay. do samosa aur ek packet wills dena.**
I see. That's fine. Two samosas and a pack of Wills cigarettes, please.

Tea seller: **haa# jii. aur kuchh chaahiye?**
Yes sir. Anything else?

Tourist: **nahii#, nahii#, bas.**
No, no, (that's) enough.

Remember, there is no 'th' sound in Hindi; when we put TH in capitals, you should sound it like a 't', but with more 'h' (think of "T'hell with it"!). Read the following notes on how to pronounce words in the dialogue.

Pronunciation

chaay	rhymes with 'fly'. Think of the 'Chi' in 'Chinese'.
garam	like 'ga+ram'.
anjii	like 'Angie', with the last syllable stressed.
kitne	like 'kit+ne'.
paise	rhymes with 'racer'.
hay	like 'hay' or 'hey'.
ek	rhymes with 'peck'.
rupeya	like 'ru+pee+ya' (stress on the first syllable).
achchhaa?	rhymes with 'thatcher'.
dena	rhymes with '(Gloria) Gaynor'.
yeh	rhymes with 'say'.
kyaa	like 'key+yah' (squashed into one sound).
do	like 'doe' (not 'do').
THiik hay	like 'T.K.'.
aur	like 'or' but with a stronger 'r' sound.
haa#	rhymes with 'car', but with a longer 'a' sound, said through the nose.
jii	rhymes with 'see', like letter 'G'.
kuchh	rhymes with 'butch'.
chaahiye	like 'chaay+e+yeh' or 'Chi'[nese]+'E.A.'.
nahii#	if spoken fast, like 'neigh'; if spoken slowly, like 'na+he'. The 'he' is spoken through the nose.
bas	rhymes with 'ass'.

Fluency practice

1. Repeat all the tourist's phrases, ten times, so fast that each sounds like one word: for example, **chaaykitnapaisehay?** ('Chi-kit-na-pacer-hay').
2. Try to say the whole dialogue in less than 20 seconds.

Structure notes

1.1 anjii!
Hello, excuse me.

This is an exceedingly popular and polite way to launch any shopping conversation. Say it confidently and loudly to attract attention, and local people will think you are a fluent Hindi speaker!

1.2 chaay kitne paise hay?
How much is tea?

Literally, this translates as 'Tea how much money is?' (there are 100 paise in one rupee). The reply you hear is:

chaay ek rupeya hay.
Tea is one rupee.
(literally 'Tea one rupee is'.)

You can also use the shorter forms, **chaay kitne hay** or **chay kitne?**

Note that **hay** (the verb) always comes last in the Hindi sentence.

1.3 Numbers 1–10

1	**ek**	like 'ek'.
2	**do**	remember that this rhymes with 'doe', rather than 'do'.
3	**tiin**	like 'teen'.
4	**chaar**	like 'char(lady)'.
5	**paa#ch**	rhymes with 'branch' (but nasalised 'aa').
6	**chhe**	like 'Che (Guevara)' but with a stronger 'h' sound.
7	**saat**	rhymes with 'art'.
8	**aaTH**	like 'art'.
9	**nao**	like 'now'.
10	**das**	rhymes with 'ass'.

Exercise 1

With a partner (if possible), ask and answer how much all of these things are. When you've worked through the whole exercise, change the prices and do it again. For example:

a) chaay (1 rupee)
<u>**chaay** kitna paise hay?</u>   <u>**chaay ek** rupeya hay.</u>

b)	special chaay	2 rupees
c)	coffee	3 rupees
d)	pepsi	6 rupees
e)	bisleri/mineral water	10 rupees
f)	glucose biscuit	4 rupees
g)	coconut biscuit	5 rupees
h)	7-Up	7 rupees
i)	Wills (cigarettes)	8 rupees
j)	Four Square (cigarettes)	9 rupees

1.4   achchhaa?
I see./ Really?/ Is that so?

The word **achchhaa?** describes all of these phrases and is very popular in India. If anyone tells you anything in Hindi, reply **achchhaa?**

1.5   ek chaay, dena.
One tea, please.

Note that **dena** is a polite way to say 'give', so you don't need a separate word for 'please'. Remember the word order for use in other phrases: number (one)/item (tea)/ **dena** (give-please).

The Hindi word for 'thanks' (**dhanyavaad**) is formal and never used in shopping conversations; Hindi speakers don't thank each other when they buy or sell things. You can say thanks in English if you wish.

Exercise 2

Three customers each want something different from the shop. Using a) as a model, fill in the gaps against b), c) and d).

a) *Customer wants:*
   Four teas and one packet of coconut biscuits.
   Customer says:
   chaar chaay dena, ek packet coconut biscuit dena.

b) *Customer wants:* Three coffees.
   Customer says: … **dena.**

c) *Customer wants:* Two packets of glucose biscuits.
   Customer says: … **dena.**

d) *Customer wants:* One Pepsi.
   Customer says: … **dena.**

1.6   yeh kyaa hay?   yeh samosa hay.
     What is this?   *This is a samosa.*
     ('This what is?')   ('This samosa is'.)

The literal translation (in brackets) shows how the subject ('This') precedes the object (samosa), with the verb (**hay**) following.

All cheap North Indian vegetarian restaurants sell most of the following dishes. All the curries are in big, unlabelled pots, so you must point and ask.

chaawal	3 rupees (rice)
chapaatii	1 rupee
daal	2 rupees
daal fry	3 rupees
aaluu gobhii	4 rupees (potato & cauliflower)
aaluu matar	5 rupees (potato & peas)
matar paniir	6 rupees

Exercise 3

a) Using the list in Structure note 1.6, ask what everything is and give an answer. For example:

Tourist: **yeh kyaa hay?**
Waiter: **yeh <u>daal</u> hay.**

b) Ask and answer how much each item is:

Tourist: **yeh kitna paise hay?**
Waiter: **yeh <u>do rupeya</u> hay.**

As an optional extension of this exercise (for which no answers are given), order some items for a meal:

Tourist: **do daal, dena.** *Two daals, please.*

If you get some bad food, you can say **yeh kyaa hay?** Using an angry tone of voice, this translates as "What (the hell's) this?".

Instead of **chapaatii** you may hear **rotii** (which rhymes with 'goatee', not 'dotty'), meaning any kind of bread: **tandoorii rotii** is baked in an oven (tandoor), while **double rotii** or **pow rotii** is western-style bread.

Food can often be ordered by the plate or half plate, e.g. **ek plate aaluu gobhii (dena)**, or **ek half plate chaawal (dena)**.

1.7 aur
and
(remember to say the 'r' strongly – 'orrrr'.)

So, to link **ek chaay, dena** *(One tea, please)* and **ek samosa, dena** *(One samosa, please)*, you say: **ek chaay aur ek samosa dena** *(One tea and one samosa, please)*. Note that **aur** is spoken quickly and quietly here.

Exercise 4

Fill in the blanks, as we've shown in the first example:

a) **ek daal fry aur chaar chapatii, dena**
   (1 dal fry and 4 chapati)
b) ... **aur** ..., **dena** (1 peas + cheese and 1 rice)
c) ... **aur** ..., **dena** (3 dal, 2 rice)
d) ... **aur** ... **aur** ..., **dena** (1 potato cauliflower, 1 dal,
   4 chapati)
e) ... **aur** ..., **dena** (2 coffees, 1 packet coconut biscuits)

1.8 THiik hay.
Fine./All right./Correct./OK.

This can be a question or an answer, depending on the tone
of voice. For example:

chaay THiik hay? *Is the tea OK?*
chaay THiik hay. *The tea's OK.*

You can also use it to greet people informally. This is very
popular:

THiik hay? *All right?*
THiik hay. *Yes, I'm all right.*

Practise asking the junior staff in your hotel, **THiik hay?**, at
every opportunity. Make it more friendly by adding **bhaaii**
(meaning 'brother', and also a friendly term for all men, like
'mate') or **diidii** ('sister', and a polite term for all women).

1.9 bhaaii diidii
brother sister

bhaaii sounds like 'buy+ee', but with a strong 'h' sound;
diidii sounds like 'deedee'. Practise saying **THiik hay
bhaaii?** *(All right, mate?)* and **THiik hay diidii?** *(OK, sister?)*.

You can add **bhaaii** before or after any shopping phrase to make it more friendly and to make your Hindi sound more natural. For example:

a) **chaay kitna paise hay, bhaaii?** or ...
   bhaaii, chaay kitne paise hay?

b) **ek chaay dena, bhaaii!** or ...
   bhaaii, ek chaay dena.

c) **yeh kyaa hay, bhaaii?** or ...
   bhaaii, yeh kyaa hay?

Repeat any ten of these expressions, adding **bhaaii**, until it feels natural. (You could add **diidii** if you want, but few Indian women work in restaurants.)

To call someone whose name you don't know, say **oh bhaaii!** *(Oi, mate!)* for men (informally). For women, **oh diidii!** *(Oi, sister!)* is used formally or informally. This means the same as **anjii** (see Structure note 1.1), but **anjii** can be used for men and women and is more polite than **bhaaii** or **diidii**. You could just hiss, but this is fairly rude.

When getting a rickshaw or taxi, settle the price first unless the driver offers to use the meter, which is unusual. You say:

Q: **New Delhi station kitne paise hay?** *How much to New Delhi station?*
A: **das rupeya.** *Ten rupees.*
Q: **saat rupeya, THiik hay?** *Is seven rupees OK?*
A: **THiik hay.** *OK (you hope).*

1.10 haa#jii *(yes – in particular, 'Yes, sir/madam')*
      jii nahii# *(no – in particular, 'No, sir/madam')*

In polite Hindi, **haa#** and **nahii#** *(yes* and *no)* must be accompanied by **jii**, whereas on the street just **haa#** and **nahii#** are used. It is impossible to translate **jii** exactly as it can mean *Sir, Mr* or *Madam* and adds a tone of respect.

24

Using **jii** on its own means also 'yes'. If you don't understand something someone says to you, you can reply in a puzzled voice: **jii?** (*I'm sorry, sir, I don't understand*). Note that **jii haa#** means the same as **haa#jii**, and that you'll often hear these two words run together as one.

If you don't like sweet tea, you would say: **ek chaay dena, chini nahii#** (*One tea, no sugar*). The word **chini** rhymes with 'skinny', and means 'sugar'.

You can also add **jii** after a person's name as a mark of respect: for example, **Gandhii jii**. It is positively rude to say a name without adding **jii** if the person you are speaking to is older than you.

jii is also added before or after any phrase to make it more polite:

jii tiin chaay, dena or **tiin chaay, dena jii**
Three teas, please.

jii yeh kyaa hay? or **yeh kyaa hay jii?**
What's this, please?

Since you can add it to every Hindi sentence, **jii** is the most useful and common word in polite Hindi. Practise adding it before and after any ten phrases and speak in a softer, more polite tone.

1.11 kyaa?
What ...?

There are two ways of using **kyaa**: (i) in the middle of a sentence, and (ii) at the beginning of a sentence.

(i) When you don't know what something is, or if you are not prepared to ask whether it is such-and-such a thing, you would say:

yeh kyaa hay? *What's this?* (literally 'This what is?')

(ii) Putting **kyaa** first in the sentence makes it a yes/no question. For example:

(**yeh daal hay:** *This is dal.*)
kyaa yeh daal hay? *Is this dahl?*

(**chaay ek rupeya hay:** *Tea is one rupee.*)
kyaa chaay ek rupeya hay? *Is tea one rupee?*

You must change the tone of the voice, just as in English:

(**yeh chaawal hay:** This is rice.)
kyaa yeh chaawal hay? *Is this rice?*

Generally, when quoted an outrageous price, if you reply with a disbelieving **kyaa?** it may well come down.

Often in the phrase **kyaa yeh ek rupeya hay?** (*Is this one rupee?*), the **kyaa** is dropped altogether, leaving only the tone of the voice to show that it is a question rather than a statement – just as in English. For example: **yeh ek rupeya hay?** (*This is one rupee?*).

1.12 Negatives

To make a negative you simply replace **hay** with **nahii#**, or, to be more formal, you put a **nahii#** before the **hay**. Look at the following examples:

yeh chaay hay. *This is tea* (literally 'This tea is').
yeh chaay nahii#. *This isn't tea* ('This tea not'). Or:
yeh chaay nahii# hay. *This isn't tea* ('This tea not is').

When you feel comfortable saying these, practise saying: 'This isn't daal, it's daal fry', etc. in Hindi.

1.13 aur kuchh chaahiye?
   Would you like anything else? or
   Do you need anything else?
   (literally 'More some wanted'.)

aur has two meanings, one of which ('and') you should have already learned in Structure note 1.7. In that context it is unstressed and appears in the middle of a sentence. Its other meaning is 'more', in which case it is stressed, and can be placed (i) first, or (ii) last in the sentence.

(i) Put **aur** at the beginning to make an offer. For example, waiters will ask you:

aur coffee chaahiye? *Would you like more coffee?*
aur chapaatii chaahiye? *Would you like more chapatis?*

(For the reply to these questions, refer to the following Structure note 1.14.)

(ii) Put **aur** at the end to make an order. Notice the word sequence (number/item/'more') in the following examples:

ek chaay aur! *(Give me) one more tea, please.*
do chapaatii aur! *(Give me) two more chapatis, please.*

You could also say **do chapaatii aur <u>dena</u>** (literally 'two breads more <u>please give</u>') or **do chapaati aur <u>chaahiye</u>** ('two breads more <u>needed</u>'), though it is more natural and easier to leave out **dena** or **chaahiye**.

1.14 chaahiye?
    needed/wanted?

This will usually be spoken to you, not by you. Waiters, for example, will ask:

chaawal chaahiye? *Do you want rice?*
kitne chapaaiti chaahiye? *How many chapatis do you want?*

To answer 'yes' you would say:
(haa# jii) ek chapaatii chaahiye.
Yes, I need one chapati.
(literally 'Yes, sir, one chapati needed').

Or, to answer 'no':
(jii nahii#) chapaatii nahii# chaahiye.
No, I don't need chapati.
('Sir no, chapati not needed').

So, **ek chapaatii chaahiye** means the same as **ek chapaatii dena**, but **dena** is easier to say.

In view of the number of persistent salesmen in India, it is vital to learn **nahii# chaahiye (bhaaii)**, *We don't want any (mate)*. A ruder response is to spit out **nahii#!** or **kuchh nahii# chaahiye!**, *We don't want anything!* (literally 'No! Some not wanted!'). It is easy to reply in English when you've been pestered in English, but speaking in Hindi is far more effective! So ...

"Hello, would you like a carpet?"
Reply: **carpet nahii# chaahiye bhaaii**.
"Very good price."
Reply: **nahii# chaahiye!**
"How about silk?"
Reply: **kuchh nahii# chaahiye!**
"Hello, rickshaw?"
Reply: **nahii#.**

Unfortunately, **nahii# chaahiye** will be the first words you need in India. On leaving Delhi airport you will be surrounded by taxi drivers and hotel commission agents all eager to sell you their overpriced services. If you keep on saying **nahii# (chaahiye)** they will leave you alone, and you can get on a local bus for a fraction of the price. On the other hand, if you learn enough Hindi to go off the beaten track, away from the other tourists and into the real India, you shouldn't need to fend off touts at all.

1.15 nahii# nahii# bas.
That's enough, thanks/that's all.
('No, no, enough.')

At the end of a meal, when offered more food, you reply like this. If you like, **nahii# nahii#** can be left unsaid.

1.16 hay
is/are

You have seen this word before, particularly in Structure notes 1.2, 1.6 and 1.8. If you can't translate the phrases in Exercise 5 below, you haven't learned those notes properly, so check back and then write down the translations.

You can also use **hay** to mean 'Do you have....?'. For example:

coffee hay? *Do you have coffee?* (literally, 'coffee is?')
chapaatii hay? *Do you have chapatis?*
chaawal hay? *Do you have rice?*

The answer, be it 'yes' or 'no', is easy:

haa# jii coffee hay or just **hay.** *Yes, we have coffee.*
jii nahii#, coffee nahii# (hay)
or **coffee nahii#** } *No, we don't have coffee.*
or just **nahii#**

Exercise 5

Translate these questions into English:

a) **yeh kitne paise hay?**
b) **yeh kyaa hay?**
c) **yeh daal fry hay?**
d) **yeh tiin rupeya hay?**
e) **(kyaa) chaay THiik hay?**
f) **haa# chaay THiik hay.**
g) **nahii# chaay THiik nahii# hay.**

Get to know India!

Tea

Tea (**chaay**) is an integral part of Indian daily life, except in the southern regions of the country where it is replaced by coffee. In India, tea is automatically served with both milk and sugar. Therefore, if you don't like sugar, you should say **chaay, chini nahii#** ('Tea without sugar'); such a request is so bizarre for most Indians that you may be asked **kyaa aap diabetic hay?** ('Are you diabetic?').

Possibly the best tea is to be found in Varanasi in Uttar Pradesh, where it is made with buffalo milk and still costs only one rupee (2p). There are many variations on the basic type of tea:

masala chaay – spiced with cardamom.
special chaay – made with more milk and/or spices.
adrak chaay – ginger tea, popular in the mountains.
duudh paati (milk tea) – made with tea, milk and sugar, with no water at all.

Then there's butter tea – black tea with old butter – drunk by Tibetans and Ladhakis, which is more like thin soup than tea, but excellent for that icy cold, dry climate. There are two kinds of Kashmiri tea, one green and the other a spiced black tea. Also available, though rarely drunk by Indians, are **kaali chay** (black tea without milk) and **nimbu chaay** (lemon tea).

Listen for the chaay waalas' cries at railway stations: **chaay, chaay, garam chaay!**, **chaay waala chaay!**, **buRHiya chaay** ('Nice' tea), **time pass chaay**, or simply the word **chaay** stretched out to sound like 'chaaaaayiya!'.

Chapter 2
Who are you?

Here, you'll learn some geography, how to ask about likes and dislikes, and how to say who you are and where you're from.

Dialogue 2

Indian:	**hindi aatii hay?**
	Do you speak Hindi?
Tourist:	**jii, thoRa thoRa.**
	Yes, a little.
Indian:	**aap kahaa# se hay?**
	Where are you from?
Tourist:	**ham London se hay.**
	I'm/We're from London.
Indian:	**achchhaa? India kaise lagta hay?**
	Really? How do you find India?
Tourist:	**achchhaa lagta hay.**
	I/We like it.
Indian:	**aapkaa naam kya hay?**
	What is your name?
Tourist:	**mera naam Mark hay.**
	My name is Mark.

Pronunciation

aatii	rhymes with 'fatty'.
thoRa	rhymes with 'snorer'.
aap	like 'harp' without the 'h'.

kahaa#	like 'ka+har', or like **haa#** (= 'yes') but with the 'k' in front.
se	like 'say'.
ham	like 'ham'.
kaise	rhymes with 'racer'.
lagta	like 'lug+ta'.
aapkaa	like 'aap+ka'.
naam	rhymes with 'jam'.
mera	rhymes with 'wearer'.

Fluency practice

1. Repeat the whole dialogue in less than 15 seconds.
2. Repeat each phrase so fast that it sounds like one word. For example: **hindiaatiihay?**

Structure notes

2.1 hindi aatii hay?
Do you speak Hindi?
(literally 'Hindi comes?', i.e. 'Does Hindi come to you?')

If you actually can speak the language, you answer:
jii haa#, hindi aatii hay. *Yes sir, I speak Hindi.*

But if you don't, you say:
jii nahii#, hindi nahii# aatii. *No sir, I don't speak Hindi.*

The majority of Indian languages have a similar name to the state in India where they are spoken, with simply an 'i' added. For example: Gujarat/**gujarati**; Punjab/**punjabi**; Bengal/**bengali**. Other countries' languages are the same: Japan/**japani**; Chin (China)/**chini**; Nepal/**nepali**; Angrez (England)/**angrezi**.

Of course, there are several possible answers to the question … **aatii hay?**, depending on your expertise:

Yes	**haa#, ... aatii hay.**
Some	**kuchh kuchh.**
A fair bit	**thoRa kuchh.**
A little	**thoRa thoRa.**
No	**nahii#, ... nahii# aatii.**
Not at all	**kuchh nahii#.**

2.2 aap kahaa# se hay? ham London se hay
Where are you from? I'm from London.
('You where from are? I London from are.')

The word **se** is always spoken as if joined to the word before it: e.g. **Londonse**.

Exercise 6

First, have a look at the following table:

Languages	Ramesh	Sonya	Raju	Sheila
a) **hindi**	yes	some	no	a little
b) **angrezi**	a little	yes	nothing	some
c) **gujarati**	no	nothing	some	yes
d) **punjabi**	some	no	yes	a fair bit

*From this, you will see that if Ramesh asks Sonya '**hindi aatii hay?**' she should reply '**kuchh kuchh**'. But if he asks her '**angrezi aatii hay?**', her response must be '**jii haa#, angrezi aatii hay**'. Here's the exercise which, if possible, you should do with a partner:*

1. *Make Ramesh, Sonya, Raju and Sheila ask and answer all the questions.*

2. *Look at a map of India and decide on five languages you each say you know, then ask questions to find out what they are.*

2.3   India kaise lagta hay? achchhaa lagta hay.
How do you like India? I/We like it.
('India how "fits" is? Good "fits" is.')

Note that **achchhaa** has two meanings: **achchha?** *(I see)*, and
achchhaa *(good)*. For example: **India achchhaa hay** *(India is
good)*. It is worked into question-and-answer patterns linked
to 'like' or preferences:

…kaise lagta hay? *How do you like …?*
…achchhaa lagta hay. *I like …*
achchhaa nahii# lagta. *I don't like …*

It is important to make your voice show if you like
something or not, and how strongly.

Exercise 7

*Imagine six people, each from a different Indian city: no. 1
is from Delhi; no. 2 from Madras; no. 3 from Calcutta; no. 4
from Bombay; no. 5 from Bangalore; no. 6 from Ahmadabad.*

a) *The person from Delhi wants to know where the others
come from. You have to frame the question and give the
five appropriate answers.*

b) *Assume that the six people speak their state language and
know a little of the language from a neighbouring state.
For example, no. 2 from Madras (in Tamil Nadu) will
speak Tamil and know some Telugu (spoken in nearby
Andhra Pradesh), but no Punjabi (which is spoken a long
way away). The person from Ahmadabad asks each of the
others 'Do you speak XXX?', naming the state language,
and then 'Do you speak ZZZ?', naming another language
which they may or may not know. Your exercise is to ask
these questions and to give appropriate replies, in Hindi.*

2.4 aapkaa naam kyaa hay? mera naam Mark hay.
What's your name? My name is Mark.
('You of name what is? My name Mark is.')

aapkaa or **mera** can go at the end of the sentence, so you can also say **naam kyaa hay aapkaa?** and **naam Mark hay mera.** Practise asking the people in Exercise 6 their names.

2.5 London kahaa# hay? London England me# hay.
Where is London? London is in England.
('London where is? London England in is.')

me# is pronounced like 'may' but nasalised. In speech it is joined to the word immediately before: **Englandme#.**

Exercise 8

Four people either like (+) or dislike (−) something. In the first part, be person 1 and ask the others about their likes and dislikes; then give an appropriate answer, as shown in the table:

1 asks 2: **beer kaise lagta hay?**
2 replies: **(beer) achchha nahii# lagta.**

1 then asks 2 whether he or she likes whisky, cricket, etc, and 2 replies. When you have completed the cycle, you could then give person 1's answers to the same questions.

	1	2	3	4
beer	+	−	−	−
whisky	+	+	−	−
cricket	−	−	+	+
cigarettes	+	−	+	−

Then ask your partner if he or she likes various foods, sports, etc. (These replies are not given in the key at the back.)

Exercise 9

Here, you test your partner's knowledge of Indian geography:

Ask: **Madras kahaa# hay?** Where is Madras?
Reply: **Madras Tamil Nadu me# hay.** Madras is in
Tamil Nadu.

Then, reverse the order. Ask 'Is Madras in Tamil Nadu?', *and
reply* 'Yes, Madras is in Tamil Nadu'; *or ask* 'Is Madras in
Gujarat?' *and reply:* 'No, Madras is not in Gujarat. Madras
is in Tamil Nadu.' *The* Key to Exercises *chapter has examples.*

Here is a list of the major Indian states and their main cities.
The states that include Pradesh in their name are usually
refered to simply by their initials, e.g. Uttar Pradesh is
known as 'UP'. Locate all these places on a map, then work
through Exercise 10.

State	Important City
Himachal Pradesh (HP)	Shimla
Uttar Pradesh (UP)	Agra
Madhya Pradesh (MP)	Bhopal
Andhra Pradesh (AP)	Hyderabad
Maharashtra	Bombay
Rajasthan	Jaipur
Kashmir	Srinagar
Goa	Goa
Bihar	Patna
West Bengal	Calcutta
Orissa	Puri
Kerala	Trivandrum
Tamil Nadu	Madras
Gujarat	Ahmadabad
Karnataka	Bangalore
Punjab	Ludhiana

India: states and languages

approximate southern limit of Hindi-speaking India

Get to know India!

Where is Hindi spoken?

Hindi is spoken as a mother tongue in Uttar Pradesh, Haryana, Madhya Pradesh, Rajasthan, Bihar and Himachal Pradesh. It is a second language in Punjab, Maharashtra, Gujarat, Kashmir, West Bengal and Goa, where virtually everyone speaks and understands it. Hindi is also spoken by some in northern Andhra Pradesh, Karnataka and parts of Orissa. Only in Kerala and Tamil Nadu is Hindi of no use to you (people in Tamil Nadu are actively hostile to Hindi). Due to the popularity of Hindi films, the language is widely understood in Kathmandu, the capital of Nepal, but not in the rest of the country.

The northern languages of India (Hindi, Gujarati, Punjabi, Bengali and Marathi) are closely related to each other, with similar script, pronunciation, grammar and vocabulary. The southern languages (Tamil, Malyalam, Telugu and Kannada) are similar to each other but very different to their northern counterparts. Both the northern and southern languages are derived from Sanskrit.

The map in this book is simplified. You cannot draw an exact line where people don't speak Hindi, because this depends on their education, occupation and so on. And there are hundreds of dialects, some of which claim to be separate languages. For a comparison of Hindi and Urdu, see Chapter 6.

You can use your Hindi in any of the areas north of the line shown on the map, but you'll obviously do better in places where Hindi is the mother tongue. After a while you'll be able to understand the gist of most conversations that you overhear, and, with luck, much of what is said to you personally.

Chapter 3
Greetings

Structure notes include formal and informal greetings, terms of address, how to say something's good or bad, and expressions of surprise, pleasure and annoyance.

Dialogue 3

Tourist: **namaste jii!**
Hello.

Hindu: **namaste jii.**
Hello.

Tourist: **kyaa haal hay bhaai?**
How are you, brother?

Hindu: **bas, THiik hay, aur aap?**
I'm fine, thanks, and you?

Tourist: **ham bhii THiik hay.**
I'm fine too, thanks.

Hindu: **aur aapkii biibiijii kaisii hay?**
And how is your wife?

Tourist: **biibiijii bhii THiik hay.**
My wife is fine too, thanks.

Hindu: **achchhii baat hay.**
That's good.

Tourist: **lekin hamaaraa bachchaa THiik nahii#.**
But our child isn't OK.

Hindu: **kyaa baat hay?**
What's up?

Tourist: **pet THiik nahii#.**
His stomach's not right.

Hindu: **arey! aafsos kii baat.**
Oh dear! That's a pity.

Pronunciation

namaste	like 'na+masty'.
haal	rhymes with 'pal', not 'Paul'.
bhii	like 'bee' but with a big 'h' sound.
aapkii	like 'aap+key'.
biibii	like 'bee+bee'.
kaisii	rhymes with 'racy'.
achchhii	like 'atch+he'.
baat	rhymes with 'cart'.
lekin	like 'lay+kin'.
hamaaraa	like 'hame+are+ra', with stress on 'are'.
bachchaa	like 'batch+cha'.
peT	like 'pet' but T with tongue vertically up.
arey	rhymes with 'carry'.
aafsos	like 'af(ter)+saus(age)'.
kii	like 'key'.

Fluency practice

Again, repeat the dialogue fast for fluency. You must say all the greetings in a friendly tone of voice.

Structure notes

3.1 namaste jii!

Formal greetings in India are completely different to the English system because firstly they depend on the religion of the person you're speaking to, and secondly the same greeting is used to say hello, goodbye, good morning, good afternoon and good evening.

If you are in a formal situation and you know the religion of the person whom you wish to address (this is normally obvious from their clothes), you should say:

To a Hindu: **namaste (jii)**, or **namaskaar.**
They reply **namaste** – literally 'Respect to you', i.e.
'Greetings'. Adding **jii** is optional and makes the greeting
more polite. To say 'goodbye', you also use **namaste.**

To a Muslim: **assalaam alaykum.**
They reply **vaalaikam assalaam**, or just **salaam** – literally
'May peace be upon you too', or simply 'Peace'. There's a
different word for 'goodbye': **khudaa haafiz.**

To a Sikh: **sat shrii akal.**
They reply **sat shrii akal** – literally 'Truth is eternal'.
The same is said for 'goodbye'.

These are fairly formal greetings, except for the one to a
Muslim, which is more widely used. They will be heard
only in a temple or at a family or business meeting. You are
unlikely to hear **namaste** in Delhi, where the people are
famous for being rude.

If you don't know the person's religion and the setting is
less formal, just say **hello jii** or, if shopping, **anjii.**

3.2   kyaa haal hay? (bas) THiik hay.
How are you? I'm fine.
('What condition is? Correct is.')

There are three ways to ask 'How are you?' in Hindi, but the
answer to each of them is the same: **(bas) THiik hay.** The word
bas doesn't really mean anything, but you'll often hear it said.

Exercise 10

*Without looking back at Structure note 3.1 until you need to
check your answers, say how the tourist greets (a) a Muslim,
(b) a Hindu, (c) a Sikh, and how they respond.*

All the preceding phrases are essential if you want to be friendly to people, so learn the three forms (and the whole of this chapter) particularly well:

(i)   **THiik hay (bhaaii)?** *How are you (brother)?* – to a man.
        THiik hay (diidii)? *How are you (sister)?* – to a woman.

(ii)   **kyaa haal hay (bhaaii)?** *How are you?* – to a man.
        kyaa haal hay (diidii)? *How are you?* – to a woman.

(iii)   **(aap) kaise hay?** *How are you?* – to a man.
        (aap) kaisii hay? *How are you?* – to a woman.

In Hindi, some words have an **-e** ending if referring to men, and **-ii** for women, as in example (iii): **kaise/kaisii**. Note also that **aap, bhaaii** and **diidii** are all optional but natural.

While **kaise/kaisii hay** is a genuine enquiry as to someone's health, **THiik hay** is more casual; **kyaa haal hay** falls somewhere between the two.

3.3   (bas) THiik hay aur aap?
I'm fine, and you?
('Enough correct is, and you?')

If asked how you are, this is the reply. The other person may then say: **ham bhii THiik hay**, *I'm fine too, thanks* ('I too correct am'); **bhii** means *too* or *also*. Another example:

Agra UP me# hay. *Agra is in UP.*
Varanasi bhii UP me# hay. *Varanasi is in UP too.*

3.4   THiik nahii#
isn't right/isn't correct
('correct is not')

If you have a health problem, you say: **peT THiik nahii#** – *My stomach's not right* (literally 'Stomach right is not'). Another use of the same phrase is: **yeh/chaay/bill THiik nahii#** – *It/tea/bill isn't right.*

3.5 achchhii baat hay!
That's good!
('Good thing is.')

... baat hay is a very common and very easy construction which has a number of different meanings. For example, **achchhii baat hay** *(That's good)*, or **achchhii baat nahii#** *(That's no good)*; the latter phrase is useful if someone is being particularly rude to you.

kyaa baat hay? *What's up?* (literally 'what thing is?'). This can have three different meanings, depending on the tone of voice used:

Friendly – **kyaa baat hay?** *(What's new?)*
Worried – **kyaa baat hay?** *(What's happened?)*
Excited – **wah! kyaa beat hay?** *(Wow! That's brilliant!)*

Following are some more expressions using **baat hay/baat nahii#**. Learn them perfectly, and your Hindi will sound more fluent:

aafsos kii baat (hay). *That's a pity, that's terrible.*
pukki baat hay? *Is that definite?* To which the answer is:
jii haa#, pukki baat hay. *Yes, it is.*
sehii baat hay. *That's true.* (**sehii** sounds like 'say+he' and means 'true'.)
yehii baat hay! *That's it.* (**yehii** rhymes with **sehii** and means 'this'.)
gundi baat hay! *That's a filthy thing to say.* (**gundi** sounds like 'gun+dee' and means 'dirty'.)
koi baat nahii#. *It doesn't matter.* (**koi** sounds like 'coy' and means 'any'.)
kuchh baat nahii#. *It doesn't matter.*
koi taklif nahii#. *It's no problem.* (**taklif** sounds like 'tack+lif(t)' and means 'problem'.)
koi muskil nahii# or kuchh muskil nahii#. *It's no problem.* (**muskil** sounds like 'mus(t)+kill' and means 'difficult': e.g. **tamil muskil hay, hindi muskil nahii#.** *Tamil is difficult, Hindi isn't difficult.*)

3.6 arey!
Oh dear!

This is a very popular expression of a bad surprise. Learn **arey bhaaii!**, *Oi mate, leave it out* (literally 'Oh brother') for use if someone is annoying you. Also, **arey yaar!** (*Oh, friend!*) is a good way of dealing with persistent salesmen. There are other popular words simiilar to **arey** which have no meaning but signify a good or bad surprise:

arey (bhaaii) – *Oh!* (Bad surprise)
bap re bap! – *Oh God!* (Big surprise)
wah (kyaa baat hay) – *Oh!* (Good surprise)
shabaash – *Oh!* (Good surprise)
oho! – *Oh!* (On a surprise meeting)

3.7 Terms of address

We have already seen the two most common words, **bhaaii** and **diidii** ('brother' and 'sister'). In Hindi you can address everyone as a theoretical relative, according to the difference in age between you.

(i) For someone much younger, use:
   male: **beTa** (*son*, sounds like 'better') or **chhoTuu** (like 'show+too', and means *oh little one*).
   female: **beTii** (*daughter*, sounds like 'Betty') or **behnjii** (like 'bairn+ji'; **behn** means *younger sister*).

(ii) For someone of the same age:
   male: **bhaaii**.
   female: **diidii**.

(iii) For someone older:
   male: **bhaaii sahb** (sounds like a 'Saab'; means *Sir*).
   female: **diidii**.

(iv) For someone much older than you:
   male: **sahb**.
   female: **maataajii** (sounds like 'Mata', as in Mata Hari, and means *mother*).

Exercise 11

Put the following expressions into Hindi (all of them have appeared in recent Structure notes), remembering to note any alternatives:

a) How are you? (to a woman).
b) That's good!
c) It's not difficult.
d) Varanasi is in Uttar Pradesh, too.
e) How are you? (casually, to a man).
f) I'm fine, and you?
g) That's a pity.
h) The bill isn't correct.

On every bus and train you will hear **chelo bhaaii sahb**, *Come on everybody! Move!* (literally 'move brother sir').

There are also specific religious forms of address. To call people politely, say:

sahb	to a Hindu (or any man)
khaan sahb	to a Muslim man (sounds like '(Imran) Khan')
sardarjii	to a Sikh man (like 'sir+dir+gee')
bahadur	to a Nepali (like 'ba+ha+duur')
diidii	to all women (unless much younger than you); a polite, friendly and very useful term.

3.8 Rhyming words

In some places it is popular to add meaningless rhyming words after many nouns and adjectives. Look at the following examples:

chaay-why = **chaay** (tea)
kapRe-kopRe = **kapRe** (cloth/clothes)
paani-waani = **paani** (water)

An analogy in English might be 'lovely-jovely', although in Hindi the usage is not necessarily informal. You don't need to make these rhymes yourself, but be prepared to hear them and to understand them.

As well as using meaningless rhyming words, Hindi speakers like to add a rhyming word which does have a meaning related to the first word:

ghuumna-phirna – *to wander about*
  phirnaa – *to turn*
dekh-paal karna – *to look after*
  dekhna – *to look at;* **paalnaa** – *to take care of*
TuuTii-phuuTii hindi – *broken Hindi*
  TuuTnaa – *to break;* **phuuTnaa** – *to explode*
estation me# bahut log aate-jaate hay – *many people come and go in the station*
roTi-kapRe – *bread and clothes* (i.e. life's essentials)
khaana-piina waala – *an eating-drinking one* (i.e. someone who is rich enough to enjoy life to the full)

Get to know India!

More about greetings and gestures

The various ways to greet people of different religions are shown in Structure note 3.1: if you are unsure of someone's religion, stick to 'hello'. You may well hear the Hindu greetings below, given that 80 per cent of Indians follow this creed:

raam, raam!	*God, God!*
jay siya raam!	*Victory holy God!*
raam jii kii jay!	*God 'sir' of victory!*

Unfortunately, the **raam** greetings have now taken on a political meaning, since they have been adopted by the Hindu fundamentalist party.

The word **jay** is very popular. At the river Ganges listen for people saying **ganga maai kii jay!** *(Ganges mother of victory)*. This doesn't translate well literally, so think of it as being **France kii jay!** *(Vive la France!)*; **jay** rhymes with 'day', and **maai** is one of several ways of saying 'mum' or 'mother'; you'll probably hear children screaming **amaai**!

In addition to the (non-religious) general greeting, **THiik hay**, there are several variations on this. For example:

kyaa baat hay? *What's up?* (literally, 'What thing is?'), to which the reply is **bas, kuchh nahii#**, *Nothing*.
kyaa haal (chaal) hay? (literally, 'What condition is?'), to which the reply is **bas, THiik hay** or **THiikTHaak.**

Another reply, when things aren't too good, is **chelta hay**, '(life) moves', i.e. *I'm surviving*. Note that **haal** and **chaal** rhyme with 'pal', not 'hall'. Here, **chaal** has no special meaning and is included only for the sound of it; similarly, the **THaak** in **THiikTHaak** (see Structure note 3.8). You came across **namaste** earlier in this chapter. It is the standard word of Hindu greeting, and also describes the gesture which goes with it – of putting the hands together as if in prayer. Whereas many men will offer to shake hands with you instead, women are more hesitant. Muslims may use a gesture to accompany a **salaam**, touching the forehead with the right hand. There are various other signs and body language to look out for; Indians use their hands as much as the Italians do when talking, and so should you.

- Turning the palm upwards, with fingers outstretched, and raising one or both hands is done to add emphasis: for example when someone says **vah! kyaa baat hay?!** (literally, 'Wow! What thing is?!'), i.e. *Brilliant!*

- The head waggle. This often accompanies **achchhaa?** and expresses acknowledgement, not agreement.

- Men will stick out the little finger of their left hand, meaning 'I'm going for a pee'.

- Men tapping the side of their nose means 'girls' or 'prostitutes'. (Indian women have their noses pierced.)

- Twisting a moustache upwards is often done by 'important' people, especially the police, to show off (only certain high-caste men are allowed to have a full moustache). It is also done by other people to mock a **baRa-sahb**, a 'big sir' or big-shot.

- When measuring things, Indians may stretch out one hand (palm up) and make a karate-chopping motion with the other, saying **iska kaimra itna lamba hay**, *It's this long* (literally, 'His camera this much long is').

- To get rid of beggars, people will make a dismissive upward flick with their left hand or fingers. This is a contemptuous gesture that you may not want to copy.

- Holding both your ears is a sign of remorse. Children may be told to do this.

Chapter 4
Shopping

In this chapter, you will learn how to say 'which?' and 'how much is …?', to define a choice, some more numbers, and also how to express fractions, weights and quantities.

Dialogue 4

Tourist: **oh bhaaii! ek packet Four Square dena.**
Brother, give me a packet of Four Square cigarettes.

Shopkeeper: **kaunsa Four Square chaahiye?**
Which ones would you like?

Tourist: **King Size waala kitna kaa hay?**
How much are the King Size?

Shopkeeper: **King Size waala das rupeya, aur yeh chhe rupeya hay**.
King size are 10 rupees and those are 6 rupees.

Tourist: **achchhaa? ek packet chhe rupeya waala dena**.
I see. Give me a packet of the 6 rupee ones.

Shopkeeper: **jii, aur kuchh chaahiye?**
Yes sir, anything else?

Tourist: **do-tin kela dena, achchhaa waala hay na!…**
Two or three bananas, good ones yeah?! …
… aur chini kitne paise hay?
… and how much is sugar?

Shopkeeper: **chini chhe rupeya kaa kilo.**
Sugar is 6 rupees a kilo.

Tourist: **tiin rupeya kaa chini dena.**
3 rupees of sugar, please.

Pronunciation

kaunsa	like 'clown' without the 'l', + 'sa'.
waala	like 'Wally' with an 'a' instead of the 'y'.
baara	rhymes with 'car+a'.
kela	rhymes with 'sailor'.
hay na	like 'hey+na'.
chini	rhymes with 'skinny'.

Fluency practice

1. Repeat the whole dialogue in less than 25 seconds.
2. Repeat each phrase so fast that it sounds like one word.

Structure notes

4.1 kaunsa ...?
Which ...?

Note that you can say **kaun** or **kaunsa**. Frequently someone will ask you: **kaunsa ...** (room/cigarette) ... **chaahiye?** *Which ... would you like?* (literally 'Which ... needed?'). Your reply may well include the next structure.

4.2 ... kitna kaa hay?
How much is/are ...?
('how much of is')

For example, when buying cigarettes you might ask: **King size waala kitna kaa hay?** *How much are the King Size ones?* (literally 'King size one how much of is'); **kitna kaa hay?** is the same as **kitna paise hay?** (which you learned in Structure note 1.2).

You can use **waala** a lot in Hindi. For example: **ek chaay dena, garam waala**, *One tea please, a hot one.*

You can use **waala** with adjectives:

buRa waala	*a big one*
garam waala	*a hot one*
pukka waala	*a ripe one*
chhoTa waala	*a small one*
THanDa waala	*a cold one*
kacha waala	*an unripe one*
yeh waala	*this one*
sasta waala	*a cheap one*

You can use **waala** with nouns:

do rupeya waala	*a 2-rupee one*
silk waala	*a silk one*

You can use **waala** with occupations:

rickshaw waala	*a rickshaw driver/puller*
chaay waala	*a tea seller*
Delhi waala	*a man from Delhi*

Members of the Parsee religion have evolved the custom of using their family occupation plus **waala** as a last name. So, charmingly, such names as 'Mr Sodawaterwaala' or 'Mr Contractorwaala' are common among them.

Exercise 12

*If you want a **chapaati** (bread), you want a hot one, so you say:* **ek chapaati dena, garam waala**. *What do you say if you need, or want to buy:*

a) a cheap room   **ek room chaahiye, … waala.**
b) a cotton shirt   **ek shirt chaahiye, … waala.**
c) a cold beer   **ek beer dena, … waala.**
d) a kilo of ripe tomatoes   **ek kilo tomato dena, … waala.**
e) a big coffee   **ek coffee dena, … waala.**

4.3 hay na?

Yeah?/Isn't it?
(literally 'is not')

When ordering something using **waala,** follow this with **hay na?** and your Hindi will sound much more fluent. For example:

ek pepsi dena, THanDa waala hay na?
A Pepsi, please a cold one, yeah?

hay na? is very easy and useful. It is frequently added to sentences without changing the meaning, just as some English speakers add 'know what I mean?'. However, **hay na?** is correct Hindi and is not restricted to informal use.

4.4 More numbers

Unfortunately, numbers in Hindi don't follow any logical system – they don't go 'forty-one', 'forty-two', but are all different words – so you have to learn them individually up to 100. It's not worth learning them all at this stage (how often are you going to need to say 'eighty-three'?). It is much better to memorise a hundred more useful words. You've already learned numbers 1–10 (see Structure note 1.3); below are some more, with a guide to the pronunciation.

11	**gyaarah**	'gee+are+rah'
12	**baarah**	'bar+rah'
13	**terah**	'tey+rah'
14	**chaudah**	'choe+dah'
15	**pondrah**	'pon+drah'
16	**solah**	'so+lah'
17	**satrah**	'sa+trah'
18	**aTHaarah**	'art+ta+rah'
19	**unniis**	'uu+niece'
20	**biis**	'beas(t)'
25	**pachchiis**	'patch+he's'
30	**tiis**	rhymes with 'yeas(t)'
40	**chaaliis**	'chaa+leas(t)'
50	**pachaas**	'patch+ass'

60	**saaTH**	rhymes with 'art'
70	**sattar**	'sat+are'
80	**assii**	rhymes with 'gassy'
90	**nabbe**	'nab+bay'
100	**(ek) sao**	'so'
200	**do sao**	
250	**do sao pachaas**	
380	**tiin sao assii, etc**	
1,000	**ek hazaar**	'has+are'
10,000	**das hazaar**	
100,000	**ek laakh**	'lack'
1,000,000	**das laakh**	
10,000,000	**ek karoR**	sounds like 'crore'

Go through these numbers several times, listening to the tape if you have it. Test yourself by dodging around the list, covering up the Hindi and pronunciation. Incidentally, watch out for wrongly-positioned commas in numbers written up in markets and so forth – always count the noughts!

Now, here's an interesting piece of information: Section 420 of the Indian penal code deals with fraud, so **chaar sao biis** (420) means *fake*, as in **yeh chaar sao biis hotel**, *This is a fraudulent hotel*.

Exercise 13

Put the following numbers into figures or words:

a)	**tiin sao tiis**	*g)*	113
b)	**chaar sao unniis**	*h)*	550
c)	**paa#ch sao pachaas**	*i)*	7225
d)	**ek sao biis**	*j)*	419
e)	**nao sao sattar**	*k)*	330
f)	**saat hazaar do sao pachchiis**	*l)*	970

Torn banknotes cannot be used in shops. You must change them at a bank, which is very time-consuming. Shopkeepers will try to give damaged notes to unwary foreigners, but you should (with a smile) refuse to accept them.

The word **patii**, meaning 'husband' or 'master', is used with the appropriate number to mean 'someone who is very rich'. For example: **laakhaptti** *(millionaire)* or **karoRpatii** *(billionaire)*. When bargaining you can say **ham laakhpatii nahii#**, *I'm not a millionaire*; however, a wizened old rickshaw driver may well point out: **nahii#, aap karoRpatii hay!**, *No, you are a billionaire!*

4.5 Fractions

half (0.5)	**aadha** (sounds like 'adder')
and a half	**saaRHe** (sounds like 'saa+reh')
	e.g. 3.5 = **saaRHe tiin**
three quarters of	**paone** sounds like 'pow+neh'
	e.g. 1.75 = **paone do**
and a quarter	**saava** (sounds like 'sa+wah')
	e.g. 8.25 = **saava aaTH**

You may wonder why 1.75 is **paone do**, when **do** means 'two', not 'one': this is because **paone** really means 'less a quarter' – therefore *two less a quarter*.

Now you can order quantities of things:
aadha kilo chaawal (dena) *half a kilo of rice (please)*
saaRHe tiin kilo chini *three and a half kilos of sugar*

Half a kilo, of course, is 500 grams, or **paa#ch sao gram**. There are also special words for 1.5 **(deRH)** and 2.5 **(DHaai)**, which are hard to say; much easier is **ek kilo paa#ch sao gram** *(one kilo 500 grams)*, instead of **deRH kilo**.

Most foodstuffs are sold by the kilo. As explained in Structure note 1.2, to ask about the price you say: **chaawal kitne paise hay?** *How much is rice?* The answer might be **chaawal das rupeya kaa kilo hay**, *Rice is ten rupees a kilo*).

Expensive items are sold by the 100 grams:
pista pondrah rupeya kaa sao gram hay, *Pistachios are 15 rupees a 100 grams.*

Other things are sold by numbers:
nimbuu do kaa paa#ch hay, *Lemons are 2Rs for five.*
kela ek kaa tiin, *Bananas are three for 1 rupee.*

In any Indian market, listen for traders calling out prices, and notice how the number of rupees always comes first.

Exercise 14

This exercise is largely intended for oral practice. In Hindi (a) ask how much each item is, (b) give the appropriate answer, and (c) ask for a kilo's worth. For example:

(a)	*How much are the XXX?*	**XXX kitne paise hay?**
(b)	*XXX are 6Rs a kilo.*	**XXX chee rupeya kaa kilo hay.**
(c)	*A kilo of XXX, please.*	**ek kilo XXX, dena.**

1	**aam**	mango	11Rs/kg
2	**liichii**	lychee	15Rs/kg
3	**santara**	orange	8Rs/kg
4	**muung phuli**	peanuts	2Rs/kg
5	**sev**	apples	8Rs/kg
6	**anguur**	grapes	9Rs/kg

Do the same with these four items, buying 100 grams of each:

7	**pista**	pistachio nuts	15Rs/100 g
8	**baadaam**	almonds	18Rs/100 g
9	**caajuu**	cashew nuts	16Rs/100 g
10	**khishmish**	raisins	14Rs/100 g

Exercise 15

This is a harder version of Exercise 14. Try to work at it with a friend, swapping roles when you've done the exercise once. Dodge among the items, to give the dialogue variety.

Make full sentences along the lines of the following examples, using the items and quantities shown against questions 1–5. XXX = item; YYY = number.

Tourist: **anjii! XXX hay?**   *Hello, have you got XXX?*
Seller: **haa# jii XXX hay**   *Yes, we do have XXX.*

Tourist: **XXX kitne paise hay?** (or **XXX kitna kaa hay?**)
       How much is XXX?
Seller: **XXX YYY rupeya kaa kilo/sao gram hay.**
       XXX is YYY rupees a kg/100 g.

Tourist: **achchhaa? YYY kilo kaa XXX, dena** (or **achch haa? YYY rupeya kaa XXX, dena**).
       I see. YYY kilo of XXX/YYY rupees of XXX, please.

a) 100 g pistachios, 300 g almonds, 400 g raisins.
b) 5 lemons, 1/2 kg oranges, 1 kg grapes.
c) 1 kg mangoes, 2 kg apples.
d) 1 kg lychees.
e) 3 kg rice, 1/2 kg sugar.

do kaa paa#ch!   Two rupees for five!
tiin kaa do!   Two for three rupees!

Instead of ordering by quantity, you can order by value (which is often easier): **tin rupeya kaa kela dena** *Give me 2Rs of bananas, please.*

Get to know India!

Haggling in Hindi

Firstly, it is important to learn where and when haggling is worthwhile. Generally, in restaurants or provision shops, you don't need to haggle since people will not try to rip you off. Instead, order your meal in Hindi (speaking as fast and confidently as possible) and it will be assumed that since you seem to know the language then you probably know the correct price. It is also true that the further you head off the beaten track, the less likely you are to be cheated. In reality, you will be overcharged very rarely; constantly asking the price of everything will only put you in a bad frame of mind and won't save you any significant sum of money at all.

When souvenir shopping, it is probably best to ask in a disinterested tone of voice how much an article costs; then, when the price is quoted, offer about half that amount while turning to walk out of the shop. If you are called back at the last moment, you have judged the real price correctly and can buy it. (You will probably be able to tell whether you are being abused too – in which case you can snap out **'kyaa bola?'**, *What did you say?*) If you are not called back, then you have judged the price too low and must start again. The difficulty will often be that you'll have no idea what the right price is. To remedy this, you could try hanging around the shop and listening to how much Indians are being charged.

In certain situations (such as hiring a rickshaw) it is vital to establish the correct price beforehand. On the next page are some useful bargaining terms, which should always be said in a friendly, joking tone of voice. Add **bhaaii** to any phrase, to make it sound more friendly.

kyaa? – *What?* (in a disbelieving tone when quoted the first price). You could say instead: **arey bhaaii!** (*Oi mate!*).

baaprebaap! – *Oh God/Why is it so much?*

itna mahanga kyo#? – *Why so expensive?* (Note that the 'h' in **mahanga** is almost silent.)

ham biis rupeyaa nahii# de sakte – *We can't pay 20 rupees.*

yeh to bahut mahanga hay – *That's really expensive.*

das rupeyaa THiik hay? – *Is ten rupees OK?* (if quoted a higher price).

sehii kiimat kyaa hay? – *What's the real price?*

kiimat thoRa kam karnaa – *Make the price a little less.*

tum crorepati ban baiTHa? – *You've become a millionaire?*

Possibly the best overall strategy, which can be used all over India when quoted a price or told there are no reservations or tickets available, is simply to stand there smiling.

Chapter 5
Transport

In this chapter you'll discover how to locate the correct bus or train, get a ticket and make other travel enquiries. You'll also learn how to tell the time, and why adjectives must 'agree' with the words they describe.

Dialogue 5

Tourist:	**kyaa yeh Delhi kii gaRii hay?**
	Is this the Delhi train?
1st Indian:	**pata nahii# bhaaii.**
	I don't know, mate.
2nd Indian:	**yeh Delhi kii gaaRii nahii# hay.**
	This isn't the Delhi train.
	voh laal waalii, Delhi kii gaaRii hay.
	That red one is the Delhi train.
Tourist:	**achchhii baat hay.**
	Cheers.
On the train:	
Tourist:	**kyaa yeh seat khaalii hay?**
	Is this seat empty?
Passenger:	**jii haa#, hay. aap (log) kidher jaana?**
	Yes, it is. Where are you going?
Tourist:	**ham (log) Delhi jaana, aur aap?**
	We're going to Delhi, and you?
Passenger:	**ham bhii Delhi jaana.**
	We're going to Delhi, too.
Tourist:	**anjii! Delhi kii ek ticket dena jii.**
(to conductor)	*Excuse me, could I have a ticket for Delhi, please.*
Conductor:	**yeh tiis rupeya hay.**
	It's 30 rupees.

Tourist:	**aur gaaRii kab jaaegii?**
	And when does the train go?
Conductor:	**sahRe tiin baje jaaegii.**
	It goes at 3.30pm.
Tourist:	**aur kab Delhi pahuu#chegii?**
	And when does it arrive in Delhi?
Conductor:	**aur raat ko das baje pahuu#chegii.**
	It arrives at 10pm.

Pronunciation

gaaRii	rhymes with 'Paddy'. (Don't forget that the Hindi letter we transcribe as a capital R has a flapped 'd' sound.)
pata	rhymes with 'stutter'.
laal	rhymes with 'pal'.
khaalii	like 'khhh+alley'.
kidher	like 'kid+her'.
jaana	rhymes with 'banana'.
log	like 'log'.
kab	like 'cab'.
jaaegii	like 'gi' as in 'giant' + 'ay-gy'. (This 'ay-gy' sounds almost like 'eggy', but is more drawn out to begin with.)
baje	like 'ba+jey' (rhymes with 'say').
pahuu#chegii	like 'pa+hoonch+ay-gy'.
sahRe	like 'sa+rey'.
raat	rhymes with 'art'.
ko	like 'co-'.

Fluency practice

As before, go through the dialogue again and again until you can say each phrase as quickly as possible. You must get used to listening to Hindi, as well as speaking it, for few native speakers will slow down just because you are clearly a foreigner who doesn't fully understand what they say.

Structure notes

5.1 kyaa yeh Delhi kii gaaRii hay?
Is this the Delhi train?
('What this Delhi of vehicle is?')

The word **gaaRii** means 'vehicle', and so it can also mean 'bus', 'train', 'car' or 'ox cart'. Although in the above context there's unlikely to be any confusion, you could also ask:

kyaa yeh Delhi kii bus/train hay?
Is this the Delhi bus/train?

If you haven't found your bus or train to Delhi, you'd ask:
Delhi kii bus/train/gaaRii kahaa# hay?
Where is the Delhi bus/train? Or
Delhi kii gaaRii kis platform per hay?
Which platform is the Delhi train on?

kis (*which*) sounds like 'kiss'; **per** (*at, on*) sounds like 'per'.

The answer might be:
Delhi kii gaaRii chhe number platform per hay.
The Delhi train is at platform 6.

A briefer answer is simply **chhe number**, *Number 6.*

5.2 yeh, woh
this, that

yeh and **woh** both also mean *he, she, it.*

5.3 Adjectives agree with nouns

In Hindi, all nouns are either masculine or feminine; and, as in French and many other languages, an adjective must agree with the noun it describes – except when it ends in a consonant, when it doesn't vary. This rule is exactly the same as in the verb agreement system, and it applies also to personal pronouns and the possessive 'of'.

61

Therefore, 'your' such-and-such could be **aapkaa** (masculine singular), **aapke** (masculine plural) or **aapkii** (feminine singular/plural). For example: *your name* translates into Hindi as **aapkaa naam** (**naam** being a masculine noun). In Dialogue 5 we see **Delhi kii gaaRii** – meaning *the Delhi train* (literally, 'Delhi of vehicle') – because the noun **gaaRii** (*vehicle*) is feminine.

You'll remember seeing **waala**, meaning *one*, in Dialogue 4 and Structure note 4.2, for example: **achchhaa waala**, *good ones*, **garam waala**, *hot one*, and so on. In Dialogue 5 we have **laal waalii**, *red one*: here it ends in **-ii** for the same reason as in the previous example. This might well seem confusing because you think of 'one' as a noun and 'red' as its qualifying adjective. But you should remember that what is really being said is 'that red-one vehicle'; thus, the adjective becomes 'red one', describing the noun 'vehicle' (which is feminine).

If you want to learn formal Hindi, you have to know the gender of all nouns – and whether they are honorific, oblique or plural – in order to get the correct endings. If you just want to communicate in everyday Hindi, do as many Indians do: use the **-ii** endings for nouns which are clearly feminine (girl, sister, mother, etc) and the **-a** endings for everyone else – excluding the examples given above (e.g. **achchhii baat** and **kii gaaRii**). This advice may irritate Hindi purists, but it is how Indians with no knowledge of English speak, and it is a much easier route for new students of Hindi to follow.

5.4   log; gujarati log
people; Gujarati people

Villagers often say **ham log** instead of **ham** for 'we', and **aap log** instead of **aap** for 'you'.

5.5   kidher jaana? ham ... jaana.
Where are you going? We're going to ...
('where going?' / 'we ... going')

This is a vital phrase, since all conversations on the train, bus or whilst walking begin with this. Another word for 'where' is **kahaa#**, so you might also hear **kahaa# jaana?**, although this is not so popular with villagers. The word **jaana** includes 'to', for example: **ham Bombay jaana** = *we're going to Bombay*. Here's a short exercise using the more common expression:

Exercise 16

Four people are going to different places. What do they say to each other? Give both the question and reply. (It's easy enough when you write these down, but see how quickly you can complete the exercise orally.)

1. Agra   2. Delhi   3. Kanpur   4. Calcutta

5.6 Delhi kii ek ticket denajii.
   One ticket for Delhi, please.
   ('Delhi of one ticket please give a'.)

Most ticket officials speak English, especially those in train stations, so don't worry if you haven't learnt the right Hindi. You can also use English words in your Hindi sentence. Besides 'ticket', used in the above example, you can also use 'first class' or 'air conditioned' (often shortened to 'AC').

Indian train station ticket clerks are usually stressed and busy, and, whether you're speaking Hindi or English, you must be patient and polite. If you are pushy and obnoxious you will simply be sent to another office.

5.7 kab jaaegii?
   When will the train go?
   ('when will go?')

kab Delhi pahuu#hegii?
When will it reach Delhi?
('when Delhi will arrive?')

We have seen **jaana**, *going*. The stem of the verb (the first part, **jaa-**) never changes, but the ending does (**-na, -egii**) to show if it is in the present tense, or future, etc. Because a **gaaRii** is female, the singular female future ending is used: **-egii**. But for now, just learn **jaaegii** and **pahuu#chegii** (the future form is fully explained later).

5.8   kitne baje hay? (or **time kyaa hay?**) **tiin baje hay.**
What's the time? It's three o'clock.

baje means 'bells' or 'rings', thus **kitne baje hay?** is literally 'how much bells (o'clock) is it?'. Telling the time in Hindi is easy, if you know all the numbers and a few new words. As you can see from the following examples, it isn't essential to include **baje** every time.

For 'half past', use **sahRe** plus the number:
   sahRe chaar (baje), *4.30*; **sahRe das (baje)**, *10.30*.
For 'quarter past', use **savaa** plus the number:
   savaa chhe, *6.15*; **savaa do**, *2.15*.
For 'quarter to', use **paone** plus the coming number:
   paone do, *1.45*; **paone tiin**, *2.45*.
For 'minutes past', say the numbers for hours and minutes:
   das chaaliis, *10.40*; **saat biis**, *7.20*.

If you want to specify 'am' or 'pm', say:
subah ko: in the morning (5–10am)
din ko: in the day (10am–5pm)
shaam ko: in the evening (5–8pm)
raat ko: at night (8pm–5am)

For example:
subah ko chhe baje, *6am* (literally 'morning for six o'clock')
din ko das baje, *10am*
sham ko saat baje, *7pm*
raat ko nao baje, *9pm*

Pronunciation

savaa	sounds like 'sa+wah'.
paone	rhymes with 'downy'.
sham	like 'sham'.
din	like 'din'.
subah	rhymes with 'tuba'.

Exercise 17

Translate the following times into Hindi and English respectively:

1.	6.30am	*a)*	**raat ko baara baje**
2.	8.45pm	*b)*	**subah ko sahRe nao baje**
3.	10.15am	*c)*	**din ko chaar das**
4.	3pm	*d)*	**din ko tiin baje**
5.	4.10pm	*e)*	**tiin baje**
6.	9.30am	*f)*	**subah ko saava das baje**
7.	12 noon	*g)*	**raat ko paone nao baje**
		h)	**subah ko sahRe chhe baje**

Below are various other words and phrases which relate to time:

ghunTa	*hour* (it rhymes with 'hunter')
adha ghunTa ke baad	*after half an hour* (literally 'number hour (of) after')*
das minute ke baad	*after 10 minutes/10 minutes later*
ek minute	*just a minute/wait a minute*

If the train or bus is about to depart, you'll hear the cry **abhii, abhii** *(Now)*, which is repeated for emphasis.

Exercise 18

Do a translation of this exchange between a tourist and a railway ticket clerk, relating to the timetable below (Delhi column). Then, make up a similar dialogue for the other destinations.

Tourist: **Delhi kii ek ticket kitne paise hay?**
Clerk: **ek sao das rupeya hay.**

Tourist: **achchhaa? ek ticket dena jii.**

Tourist: **Delhi kii gaaRi kab jaaegii?**
Clerk: **Delhi kii gaaRii subah ko chhe baje jaaegii.**

Tourist: **aur kab Delhi pahuu#chegii?**
Clerk: **din ko sahRe chaar baje pahuu#chegii.**

Tourist: **aur Delhi kii gaaRii kis platform per hay?**
Clerk: **Delhi kii gaaRii chhe number platform per hay.**

	Delhi	Bombay	Agra	Kanpur	Jaipur	Jodpur
Dep.	6am	8.15pm	11.30pm	10am	9am	11.15am
Arr.	4.30pm	7.30pm	5am	2pm	1.30pm	2.45pm
Plat.	6	2	7	8	4	1
R's	10	120	50	40	20	30

Get to know India!

Trains in India

For any long journey, try to travel by train. The Indian rail
network is one of the most extensive in the world and offers
a wonderful window on the country and its people. You
can buy 1st class (air-conditioned or otherwise), 2nd class
(reserved or unreserved), and unreservable 2nd class, which
is absolute bedlam. A 2nd class sleeper, air-conditioned, is
probably the best value. To travel cheaper than this (i.e. with
no reservation) is chaotic, while the more expensive option
may leave you feeling rather isolated. On some trains the
fare includes food as well, and bedding rolls can be
reserved for an extra fee.

No one ever forgets the first time they see an Indian
train pull into a station. Hordes of passengers get on and
off, accompanied by red-shirted, wizened porters with
impossible piles of suitcases on their heads. Beggars and
vendors (of tea, cigarettes, papers, etc) roam along the
corridors or beneath the windows, each with their own
distinctive cry. Although it looks like chaos, you'll eventually find your name and berth on a computer printout,
pasted on your carriage. It's wise to get to the station an
hour before the train is due to leave, in order to check your
seat reservation.

You must keep an eye on your luggage, especially at
arrival and departure time. Thieves are likely to be groups of
young men in scruffy western clothes. At night use your bag
as a pillow, and/or chain it to the berth. Make friends with
the other occupants of the compartment, especially families,
and they'll watch over your luggage when you leave the
compartment. Say **'jii, iska dekh-paal karo'** (*'please look after
it'*), and people will oblige. Indeed, you will almost certainly
chat with your fellow travellers, and if you speak any Hindi,
people will be curious and pleased about that.

Chapter 6
More about yourself

Structure notes in this chapter include asking questions, use of verbs and how gender affects endings.

Dialogue 6

Indian: **shaadii kiya?**
Are you married?

Male Tourist: **jii nahii#, shadii nahii# kiya.**
No, I'm not married.

Indian: **aapke koi bhaaii-behn hay?**
Do you have any brothers or sisters?

Male Tourist: **haa# jii, hay.**
Yes, I do.

Indian: **kitne bhaaii hay?**
How many brothers do you have?

Male Tourist: **mere ek buRe bhaaii, aur ek chhoTa.**
I have one big brother and one younger brother.

Indian: **aur kitnii behn hay?**
And how many sisters do you have?

Male Tourist: **merii koi behn nahii#.**
I don't have any sisters.

Indian: **maata pita jii THiik hay?**
Are your mother and father OK?

Male Tourist: **jii haa# maata pitaa jii THiik hay.**
Yes, my mother and father are fine.

Indian: **aapkaa rozghaar kyaa hay?**
What's your occupation?

Male Tourist: **jii, ham nahii# samajhte.**
Sorry, I don't understand.

Indian:	**matlub, aap kyaa kaam karte hay?**
	I mean, what job do you do?
Male Tourist:	**ham office me# kaam karte hay. ham secretary hay.**
	I work in an office. I'm a clerk.
Indian:	**aur kitne paise milte hay?**
	And how much do you get?
Male Tourist:	**aaTH hazaar rupeya milte hay.**
	I get Rs8000.
Indian:	**aap kitne saal ke hay?**
	How old are you?
Male Tourist:	**ham tiis saal ke hay.**
	I'm 30.

Pronunciation

shaadii	rhymes with 'caddy'.
kiya	like 'key+yah'.
mere	like 'mare+eh'.
buRe	rhymes with 'rudder'.
chhoTa	rhymes with 'floater'.
kitnii	like 'kit+knee'.
merii	like 'Mary'.
bas	rhymes with 'pass'.
maata	like 'mat+ah'.
rozgaar	like 'rose+gar'.
samajhte	like 'some+madge+ta'.
matlub	like 'matt+lub'.
karte	like 'carter'.
pitaa	like 'pitta (bread)'.

Fluency practice

Keep on reading the dialogue until you can repeat it quickly. Act it out with a friend, or at least say the words aloud. And remember to listen: train your ear as well as your mouth!

Structure notes

6.1 **shaadii kiya?**
Are you married?
('Marriage made?')

Your answer to this question could be:
jii ha#, shaadii kiya.
Yes, I'm married.

A negative answer would be:
jii nahii#, shaadii nahii# kiya.
No, I'm not married.

If yes, you may then be asked:
aapke koi bachche hay?
Do you have any children?
('yours any children are?')

Answer:
jii nahii#, mere koi bachche nahii#.
No, I don't have any children. Or
jii haa# mera ek luRka hay aur ek luRkii.
Yes, I have one boy and one girl.

6.2 **aapke koi bhaaii-behn hay?**
Do you have any brothers or sisters?
('Yours any brothers-sisters are?')

mere ek buRe bhaaii hay.
I have one big brother.
('Mine one big brother is.')

As the two preceding sentences demonstrate, to say 'I have' in Hindi you must use **hay** – hence the need for convoluted literal translations using 'are' or 'is'. Here's another example:

mere do bhaaii hay.
I have two brothers.
('Mine two brother are.')

6.3 kitne bhaaii hay?   kitnii behn hay?
   How many brothers   How many sisters
   (do you have)?   (do you have)?

Note how the ending of **kitne** changes to **kitnii** because it refers to a woman. Look at **mere ek buRe bhaaii** (Structure note 6.2) and **merii koi behn nahii#** (Dialogue 5): we use **mere** because it refers to a man, and **merii** because it refers to a woman.

So, in the following words (adjectives/pronouns) we see the same spelling change according to gender; **-e** for men, **-ii** for women:

kitne, kitnii ...?   *how many ...?*
mere, merii   *mine*
buRe, buRii   *big, old*
chhoTe, chhoTii   *small, young*

To complicate matters, there are two masculine endings:
mer<u>a</u> for the singular (or non-honorific), and
mer<u>e</u> for the plural (or honorific).

These adjectives must agree. However, in street Hindi you can say **mera/mere** just the same and it's quite acceptable; it's much more important to speak quickly.

You'll need to learn these new words before working on the next exercise:

aapke   *yours* (used when talking politely
             to adults)
tumhaare   *yours* (when talking to children; like
             'tum+har+reh')
dusre   *the other* (like 'do+s+ra')
sab   *all* (rhymes with 'cab')
dono#   *both* (like 'don+oh')

Also remember how word endings change for males and females: tumhaare/tumhaarii; buRe/buRii; chhoTe/chhoTii; kitne/kitnii.

Exercise 19

Ask the children in this family about their brothers and sisters, and give the appropriate replies: Ramesh (aged 5), Raja (8) and Anil (12) are boys, while Sonya (6) and Puja (10) are girls. Follow this question-and-answer pattern:

Ramesh
1. **tumhaare kitne bhaaii hay?** *How many brothers do you have?*
1a. **mere do bhaaii hay.** *I have two brothers.*
2. **buHre ki chhoTe?** *Younger or older?*
2a. **dono# buRe hay.** *They're both older.*
3. **aur tumhaarii kitnii behn hay?** *And how many sisters do you have?*
3a. **meri do behn hay.** *I have two sisters.*
4. **buRii ki chhoTii?** *Older or younger?*
4a. **dono# buRe hay.** *They're both older.*

Sonya
1. **tumhaare kitne bhaaii hay?** *How many brothers do you have?*
1a. **mere tiin bhaaii hay.** *I have three brothers.*
2. **buRe ki chhoTe?** *Older or younger?*
2a. **do buRe hay, aur ek chhoTa.** *Two are older, one is younger.*

And so on. Complete the exercise for Sonya and the other children. Then, for additional practice, create your own families or add new children to this one.

6.4 **pitaa jii**
father
('father sir')

jii is always added to **pitaa**, in order to show respect. For the same reason, it is also added to **maataa** (*mother*) and **biibii** (*wife*).

6.5 **jii, ham nahii# samajhte.** (Said by a man.)
    jii, ham nahii# samajhtii. (Said by a woman.)
    Sorry, I don't understand.
    ('Sir, I not understand'.)

This is a very useful phrase! Note the masculine/feminine variation: **samajhte, samajhtii.** Verb endings often change like this. Learn the verbs below, then see how the same gender distinction is made in the next structure:

kar	*do* (sounds like 'car')	
jaan	*know* (sounds like 'Jan')	
reh	*live/stay* (sounds like 'rare')	} + **te/tii**
pii	*drink/smoke* (sounds like 'pea')	
mil	*get* (sounds like 'mill')	

Male: **ham school me# kaam karte (hay)**
           I work in a school
Female: **ham office me# kaam kartii (hay)**
           I work in an office
Male: **ham hindi jaante**
           I know Hindi
Female: **ham punjabi jaantii**
           I know Punjabi
Male: **ham Delhi me# rehte**
           I live in Delhi
Female: **ham Agra me# rehti**
           I live in Agra

6.6 **aap kyaa kaam karte (hay)?**
    What job do you do?
    ('You work what do is?')

It's **karte** (sounds like 'carter') because the tourist is a man. Were she to be a woman it would be **kartii** (which sounds like 'car+tea'). All verbs in the present tense must end in **te** or **tii**. Generally, you include **hay** in a question but not in a statement or negative; this, however, is flexible. When you want to describe what you do for a living, use **ham ... hay** and the English word for your job: **ham** (secretary) **hay**, *I'm a secretary* (literally 'I (occupation) am').

73

You may be asked **kitne paise milte hay?** *How much (money) do you get?* Here, the **te** stays the same for men and women because the subject of **milte** is **paise**, which is masculine. If the verb ends in **na** (as in **karna/dena**) it doesn't change.

In India, wages are calculated by the month (**mahiine per**, *per month*). As the brackets in the following example show, these words can, in fact, be omitted:

(mahiine per) aaTH hazaar rupeya milte (hay).
I get 8000 rupees (per month).
('Month per eight thousand rupees get I.')

6.7 **aap kitne saal ke/kii hay?**
How old are you?
('You how many years of are?')

ham tiis saal ke/kii hay.
I'm 30 years old.
('I 30 years of am.')

ke is used if the subject is a man. If the subject is a woman, **ke** changes to **kii**. Note that **kitne** doesn't change because its subject is **saal**, which is masculine. For a woman, therefore, the question-and-answer pattern is:

aap kitne saal kii hay? *How old are you?*
ham biis saal kii hay. *I'm 20.*

You can ask the age of somebody's relative. For example:

aapke bhaaii kitne saal ke hay? *How old is your brother?*
woh biis saal ke hay. *He is 20 years old.*
apkii behn kitne saal kii hay? *How old is your sister?*
woh biis saal kii hay. *She is 20 years old.*

Use **woh** for a 'he' or 'she' who's not present at the conversation, and **yeh** for someone who is.

Remember that **buRe** can mean 'big' or 'old', that **chhoTa** can mean 'small' or 'young'. To compare ages, say:

mere bhaaii ham se tiin saal buRe hay.
My brother is three years older than me.
('My brother me than three years big is.')

merii behn ham se ek saal chhoTii hay.
My sister is one year younger than me.
('My sister me than one year smaller is.')

6.8 Questions

You've been shown some question structures in earlier chapters; here are more examples, which use the verbs and the male/female agreement rules shown in Structure note 6.5, and lead you into the next exercise.

(i) Sonya asks Ramesh:
   Rameshjii, aap kahaa# rehte (hay)? *Where do you live?*

(ii) Ramesh replies:
   ham Delhi me# rehte hay. *I live in Delhi.*

(iii) Ramesh asks Sonya:
   Sonyajii, aap kahaa# rehtii (hay)? *Where do you live?*

(iv) Sonya replies:
   ham Agra me# rehtii hay. *I live in Agra.*

Or, 'Yes/No' answers:

Rameshjii, kyaa aap hindi jaante (hay)? *Do you know Hindi?*
jii, haa#, ham (hindi) jaante. *Yes, …*
jii nahii# ham (hindi) nahii# jaante. *No, …*

Sonyajii, kyaa aap gujarati jaantii (hay)? *Do you know Gujarati?*
jii haa# ham jaantii. *Yes, …*
jii nahii# ham nahii# jaantii *No, …*

Rameshjii, kyaa aap cigarette piite (hay)? *Do you smoke?*
jii haa# ham cigarette piite. *Yes, …*
jii nahii# ham cigarette nahii# piite. *No, …*

Exercise 20

Using the table below, which shows who lives and works where, who smokes, etc, complete the appropriate questions and answers for each person (24 sets in all). The first two questions/answers for Ramesh and Sonya are given as models. Begin your question with the person's name, and be careful to get the te/tii, ke/kii endings correct.

		A *Ramesh*	**B** *Sonya*	**C** *Sheila*	**D** *Abdul*
a)	*Lives in*	Delhi	Agra	Bombay	Agra
b)	*Works in*	office	school	bank	factory
c)	*Knows*	Hindi	Bengali	Bengali	Hindi
d)	*Smokes*	yes	no	no	yes
e)	*Salary*	1000Rs	2000Rs	3500Rs	4700Rs
f)	*Age*	25	30	20	40

For example:

a) Q: **Ramesh jii, aap kahaa# rehte hay?**
A: **ham Delhi me# rehte (hay).**
Q: Sonya jii, aap kahaa# rehtii hay?
A: **ham Agra me# rehtii (hay).**

b) Q: **Ramesh jii, aap kyaa kaam karte hay?**
A: **ham office me# kaam karte (hay).**
Q: **Sonya jii, aap kyaa kaam kartii hay?**
A: **ham school me# kaam kartii (hay).**

And so on. Here are the rest of the questions. The replies you must work out by yourself (in full, not just 'haa# jii'/'jii nahii#' for questions 3 and 4).

c) **... jii, kyaa aap [language] jaante/tii hay?**
d) **... jii, kyaa aap cigarette piite/tii hay?**
e) **... jii, kitne paise milte hay?**
f) **... aap kitne saal ke/kii hay?**

Get to know India!

Hindi versus Urdu

The difference between Hindi and Urdu is hard to define. In their everyday spoken forms the languages are virtually identical, but a philosophical debate in either tongue would be incomprehensible to a speaker of the other. Their written forms are quite dissimilar. Hindi is India's national language, while Urdu is Pakistan's.

Both Hindi and Urdu developed out of the same dialect, spoken to the west of Delhi. It was formalised into Urdu (using Arabic words and an Arabic script) by the Moghuls. In fact, Urdu was the language of the army, which was gradually refined and eventually became the language of the Moghul court. The same dialect also developed in a different direction, using words derived from Sanskrit, to become (proper) Hindi. There is therefore much common ground, to the extent that if you spoke Hindi to a Pakistani, he'd say you were speaking Urdu – whereas a north Indian would describe the same words as Hindi.

But the languages are not the same, and as you learn more, the more different they become. Words for complicated ideas are different, as are many basic words (especially those to do with the family). Hindu religious words, such as **namaste, raam raam**, and so on, are taboo in Urdu.

Hindi is also affected by politics, though more in theory than in practice, by people who wish to purge it of 'foreign' words, i.e. those not derived from Sanskrit. Hindi pundits are trying (quite unsuccessfully) to replace commonly used English words with Sanskrit-derived ones: instead of 'TV' for 'television', they'd have you say **duur-darshan**, which hardly anyone knows. Ignore these, and use the words in this book, which are spoken in everyday Hindi.

Chapter 7
Your trip in India

In this chapter you'll learn how to ask and answer more introductory questions linked to your trip in India, but which are also usable in other contexts.

Dialogue 7

Indian: **India kab aaye?**
When did you come to India?

Tourist: **ek hafta hua aaye.**
(Male) *A week ago.*

Indian: **aur India kaise aaye?**
How did you come to India?

Tourist: **ham hawaaii-jahaaz se aaye.**
I came by plane.

Indian: **aur kitne ghunTe lagta hay?**
And how long does it take?

Tourist: **das ghunTa lagta hay.**
It takes ten hours.

Indian: **aur kiraaya kitne paise hay?**
And how much is the fare?

Tourist: **kiraaya lugbhug das hazaar rupeya hay**
The fare is about 10,000 rupees.

Indian: **baap re baap!! kyo# India aaye?**
Oh my God!! And why did you come to India?

Tourist: **ghuumna-dekhna ke liye.**
To look around.

Indian: **India me# kyaa dekha? kahaa# gaye?**
What have you seen in India? Where have you been?

Tourist: **ham Agra gaye, aur Taj Mahal dekha.**
I've been to Agra, and seen the Taj Mahal.

Indian:	**aur Delhi me# kahaa# rehte hay?**
	And where do you stay in Delhi?
Tourist:	**ham Gandhi Guesthouse me# rehte hay.**
	I stay in the Gandhi Guesthouse.
Indian:	**Delhi me# kab se rehte hay?**
	How long have you been in Delhi?
Tourist:	**do din se (ham Delhi me# rehte hay).**
	(I've been in Delhi) for two days.
Indian:	**aur kab tak rehenge?**
	And how long will you stay?
Tourist:	**ham ek hafta tak rehenge.**
	I'll stay one week.
Indian:	**aur India me# kyaa karenge? kahaa# jaaenge?**
	And what will you do? Where will you go?
Tourist:	**ham Varanaasi jaaenge.**
	I'll go to Varanaasi.

Pronunciation

aaye	like 'eye+yeh'.
jahaaz	like 'je+has'.
kiraaya	ike 'ki+rye+ah' (stress on 'rye').
kyo#	like '(To)kyo', but nasalised.
ghuumna	rhymes with '(r)oom' + 'na'.
dekhna	like 'deck+na'.
dekha	like 'deck+a'.
ke liye	like 'ke+lee+eh'.
gaye	like 'guy+eh'.
rehte	like 'rare+teh'.
tak	halfway between 'tack' and 'tuck'.
rehenge	like 'ruh+heng+eh'.
karenge	like 'kuh+reng+eh'.
jaaenge	like 'ja+yeng+eh'.

Fluency practice

As usual, repeat the dialogue phrase by phrase.

Structure notes

7.1 India kab aaye?
When did you come to India? (to a man)
('India when came?')

India kaise aaye?
How did you come to India? (to a man)
('India how came?')

Because a man is speaking, and being spoken to, the verb must end in **-e** to show that the subject is male. Had the subject been a woman, the verb would have ended in **-ii**. In the past tense only the verbs **aaye/aayii** *(came)* and **gaye/gayii** *(went)* have different endings for men and women; other verbs keep the **-e** ending for both sexes.

If you say 'we' referring to a man and a woman together (or even one man and 20 women), you use the male voice. Sexist, but true. See the Grammar section for more details on verb endings.

7.2 ek hafta hua aaye.
We/I came a week ago.
('One week was came.')

To say 'ago' in Hindi, you use a number (one, two, etc) and then the unit of time (week, month, etc) plus **hua** *(was)*: **do hafta hua**, *two weeks ago*. Or you can say **do hafta pehle**, *two weeks before*. For the future: **tiin din ke baad**, *after three days*.

Learn the time units and 'before'/'after':

day	**din**	(sounds as in 'dinner', not as in 'Dean').
week	**hafta**	(like 'have to' spoken very quickly).
month	**mahiine**	(sounds like 'muh+he+neh').
year	**saal**	(rhymes with 'pal', not 'Paul').
before	**pehle**	(sounds like 'pair+lay').
after	**ke baad**	(like 'kay bad').

Exercise 21

Translate the following from Hindi to English and vice versa.
Write down your answers, or respond orally to the cassette or
a friend reading out the questions.

a) **das minute hua**
b) **tiin saal hua**
c) **chhe mahiine ke baad**
d) **ek mahiine hua**
e) **ek saal pehle**
f) **aaTH din ke baad**
g) **nao ghunTa hua**
h) **ek hafta ke baad**

i) after eight days
j) one month ago
k) three years ago
l) ten minutes ago
m) after one week
n) after six months
o) nine hours ago
p) one year ago/before

saal – year   hafta - week

7.3 ham hawaaii-jahaaz se aaye.
I came by aeroplane.
('We air-ship by came.')

Here, notice firstly that **ham** can mean either 'we' or 'I', and
secondly that **se** can have three different meanings:

se = *from*: **ham London se hay.**
            I'm from London.
se = *than*: **mere bhaaii ham se ek saal buRe hay.**
            My brother is one year younger than me.
se = *by*:   **ham bicycle se aaye.**
            I came by bicycle.

7.4 kitne ghunTa lagta hay?
How long does it take?
('how many hours "fits" is?')

kitne paise lagta hay?
How much does it cost?
('how much money "fits" is?)

You've met **lagta hay** before – it first appeared in Structure note 2.3, translating as *like*. It has a different meaning in this new context, but the main thing to note here is that **lagta hay** does not change, whether spoken by men or women.

To add to these structures details such as place names and mode of transport, you need **se** (which means *from, by, than*) and **jaana** (literally 'going to'). For example:

Bombay se Delhi jaana, bus se, kitne ghunTa lagta hay?
How long does it take from Bombay to Delhi by bus?
('Bombay from Delhi going [to], bus by, how many hours "fits" is?')

The answer might be:
das ghunTa (lagta hay), *(It takes) ten hours.*

Exercise 22

The following table shows fares and journey times from Bombay to Delhi, Madras and Calcutta (but don't take these as being spot-on accurate!) Using the same question-and-answer routine as in Structure note 7.4, ask "How much" and "How long" to each destination by plane and bus, and then give the apppropriate reply.

From Bombay to:	Delhi	Madras	Calcutta
1. (by plane) cost Rs	2000	4500	3000
2. time in hours	3	4¹/₂	3¹/₂
3. (by bus) cost Rs	200	350	300
4. time in hours	10	14	12

When you've asked and replied to these questions, get out your map of India and make up some more. Such practice is essential in achieving fluency and general confidence; it doesn't matter that you've no idea of the true details.

7.5   kyo#?
Why?

If you are asked any question beginning with **kyo#**, you can always reply **kyo# nahii#**, *Why not?* However, a more informative reply is:

Taj Mahal dekhna ke liye.
To see the Taj Mahal.
(literally 'Taj Mahal see in order to.')

Exercise 23

Below is a list of Indian state capitals and the language spoken in each state. Imagine someone visits each city, to learn the local language. Ask him or her why he/she came. For example:

kyo# Calcutta aaye?   *Why did you come to Calcutta?*
Bengali siikhna ke liye.   *To learn Bengali.*

Shimla (HP)	Hindi
Agra (UP)	Hindi
Bhopal (MP)	Hindi
Hyderabad (AP)	Telugu
Bombay (Maharashtra)	Marathi
Jaipur (Rajasthan)	Hindi
Srinagar (Kashmir)	Kashmiri
Goa (Goa)	Konkani
Patna (Bihar)	Hindi / Bihari
Calcutta (West Bengal)	Bengali
Puri (Orissa)	Oriya
Trivandrum (Kerala)	Malayalam
Madras (Tamil Nadu)	Tamil
Ahmadabad (Gujarat)	Gujarati
Bangalore (Karnataka)	Kannada

Note the object/verb order here, followed by **ke liye**.
Here are some other examples:

ghuumna-dekhna ke liye (*in order*) *to wander and look,*
to sightsee
hindi siikhna ke liye (*in order*) *to learn Hindi*

7.6   India me# kyaa dekha?
What have you seen in India?
('India in what seen?')

In Hindi, to make the past tense, you use the verb stem with
-a or **-ya**. For example, **milna**, *to get*: the stem is **mil-**, so in
the past tense it is **mil<u>a</u>**.

paise mila?	*Did you get the money?*
haa#, paise mila.	*Yes, I got the money.*
nahii#, paise nahii# mila.	*No, I didn't get the money.*
siikhna	*to learn*
hindi kahaa# siikhliya?	*Where did you learn Hindi?*
Delhi me# siikhliya.	*I learned in Delhi.* (**siikhliya**, from the verb 'to learn', sounds like 'seek+lee+ah'.)
is kitab se siikhliya.	*I learned from this book.* (**is** rhymes with 'hiss', not 'is'.)

7.7   Delhi me# kahaa# rehte hay?
Where do you stay in Delhi? (said to a man)
('Delhi in where stay are?')

Delhi me# kab se rehte hay?
How long have you been in Delhi? (said to a man)
('Delhi in when from stay are?')

Again, the verb finishes in **-e** because the subject is male;
and it would be **reht<u>ii</u> hay** if the subject were female.
(Notice that Hindi uses the present tense to say 'How long
have you been here?', which translates exactly as 'How long
are you here?')

7.8   **rehenge**   *will stay*
      karenge   *will do*
      jaaenge   *will go*

The future tense is formed by adding **-enge/-engii** to the stem of a verb. For example: **dekhna** *to see;* **dekhenge** *we will see* (male). As in the present tense, the ending changes from **-e** to **-ii** if the subject is female: **rehengii, karengii, jaaengii, dekengii.**

7.9   **kab tak rehenge?**
      How long will you stay?
      ('When until will stay?')

Or: **kitne din rehenge?**
      How many days will you stay?

Either way, your reply will probably be something like the following (depending, of course, on your itinerary). Note a couple of new words: *then* = **phiir** (sounds like 'fear'); and *afterwards* = **baad me#** (like 'bad+may').

      ham das din (tak) rehenge ...
      We'll stay (until) ten days ...
      ... phiir/baad me# Agra jaaenge.
      ... then/afterwards we'll go to Agra.

Exercise 24

The table below gives details of four different itineraries: when each person arrived, how long he or she has been in Delhi, and so on. Then follows a series of questions about these details, and the replies (as given by Ramesh). You must make up similar questions for each of the other people, taking care to check that Ramesh and Anil have male endings, and Tara and Sonya female endings.

		Ramesh	Tara	Anil	Sonya
a)	Arrived:	2 months	4 weeks	6 days	9 weeks
b)	Will stay:	1 month	3¹/₂ weeks	4 months	3 days
c)	Has gone to:	Goa, Madras	Delhi, Bombay	Varanaasi	Agra
d)	Has seen:	Tamil Nadu	Old Delhi	Ganga Mai	Taj Mahal
e)	In Delhi:	2 days	1 week	1 day	6 days
f)	Stays at:	Hilton Hotel	Hotel Vikram	Gandhi	Gandhi
g)	Why came:	to learn Tamil	sightseeing	to learn sitar	why not?

Questions (to Ramesh)	Replies (by Ramesh)
a) **India kab aaye?**	**do mahiine hua aaye.**
b) **kab tak rehenge?**	**ek mahiine tak rehenge.**
c) **kahaa# gaye?**	**ham Goa aur Madras gaye.**
d) **kyaa dekha?**	**Tamil Nadu dekha.**
e) **Delhi me# kab se rehte hay?**	**ham Delhi me# do din se rehte hay.**
f) **Delhi me# kahaa# rehte hay?**	**ham Hilton Hotel me# rehte hay.**
g) **kyo## India aaye?**	**Tamil siikhna ke liye.**

Exercise 25

Look at this table of who-does-what-and-for-how-long, noting how the following questions and replies relate to Ramesh's trip. Then make up similar sentences for each of the other travellers, being careful to get the masculine and feminine verb endings correct.

		Ramesh	Raja	Sonya	Sheila	Tara
1.	Goes to	Delhi	Agra	Calcutta	Delhi	Jaipur
2.	Stays	2 weeks	1 week	10 days	2 years	5 months
3.	Goes on to	Bombay	Bombay	Puri	Agra	Madras
4.	Stays	1 month	2 weeks	4 months	1 day	5 years

1. **Ramesh jii, aap India me# kahaa# jaaenge?**
   Where will you go in India?
1a. **ham Delhi jaaenge.**
   I'll go to Delhi.
2. **aur Delhi me# kab tak rehenge?**
   How long will you stay in Delhi?
2a. **ham do hafta rehenge, phiir Bombay jaaenge.**
   I'll stay two weeks, then I'll go to Bombay.
3. **aur Bombay me# kab tak rehenge?**
   How long will you stay in Bombay?
3a. **ham ek mahiine (tak) rehenge.**
   I'll stay one month.

Now make your own schedule for India, saying where you'll go and how long you'll stay.

Get to know India!

Buses in India

Although trains are usually better for longer journeys, buses are often quicker or more convenient for short trips (in the Delhi-Jaipur-Agra triangle, for instance). There are no trains in the Himalayas, so the only means of public transport is the bus.

There are usually local council-run and private buses on major routes all over India. The former are very cheap, bumpy, noisy and crowded. The latter are more comfortable, and although their fares may be twice as much, they are still cheap. Whenever possible, reserve your seat in advance (this is compulsory on deluxe buses) and avoid the bumpier back seats.

You'll hear many set phrases on the buses. The conductor will whistle to the driver once for 'stop', twice for 'go' or will say to him: **'chelo'** (or **'chelna'/'chelo jii'**), meaning *'go'*. Passengers say **'roko'** (or **'rokna'/'roko jii'**), for *'stop'*. The conductor will constantly say **'andar chelo, andar'**, *'inside move, inside'*. To ask for your ticket, say **'ek ticket Delhi'**, *'One ticket for Delhi'*. The conductor may ask for **'khuula paisa'**, meaning that he wants the money in small change, not a big note. To ask if a seat is vacant, say **'kyaa yeh seat khaali hay?'**, *'Is this seat empty?'*, and someone will reply **'khaalii hay'** (*'It is empty'*) or **'khaalii nahii#'** (*'It is not empty'*). When the bus stops for tea, ask the conductor **'kitne minute (rokega)?'** *'How many minutes (will we stop)?'*.

If you learn to read Hindi, you'll see lots of amusing 'public information' messages written on and in the buses. For example: 'Sleeping on seats no. 1, 2 & 3 is forbidden', or 'Oh you with the evil eye, may your face be blackened' (i.e. don't drive so close).

Chapter 8
Revision

This chapter sums up what you should have learned by now, and adds a little more detail.

You'll have picked up several basic introductory questions in the preceding chapters: during your travels in India every conversation with a stranger is likely to include some of these, though not necessarily in the order given here. It is essential to be able to answer them. They will be spoken fast, so to identify each question you have to be able to pick out the important words, rather than know what every single word means.

Cover up the answers with a piece of paper, to see which ones you know and which ones you still need to practise. Remember that in questions 5, 6 and 10, the verb ending would change to **-i** if spoken by, or to, a woman.

	Question:	Reply:
1.	**hindi aati hay?**	**jii, thoRa, thoRa.**
	You know Hindi?	*A little.*
	or:	**kuchh kuchh.**
		Some.
2.	**hindi kahaa# siikh liya?**	**India me# siikh liya.**
	Where did you learn Hindi?	*In India.*
	and/or:	**is book se siikh liya.**
		From this book.

3. **yahaa# ki vahaa# siikh liya?**   **yahaa# siikh liya.**
   Did you learn (it) here or there?   *I learned (it) here.*

Note that **siikh liya** is a compound verb (**siikhaa**), which is explained in the Grammar chapter.

If you're travelling on a bus or train, or walking …

4. **kiddher jaana?**   **ham Bombay jaana.**
   Where are you going?   *To Bombay.*

5. **aap Calcutta me#**   **ham YMCA me#**
   kahaa# rehte hay?   **rehte hay.**
   Where are you staying   *In the YMCA.*
   in Calcutta?

Remember that the verb ending in example 5 (and also in 6 and 7) would change to **-ii** if spoken by or to a woman. Practise this.

6. **(aap Calcutta me#) kab**   **ham chaar din se**
   se rehte hay?   **yahaa# rehte.**
   How long have you been…   *For four days.*
   (in Calcutta)?

7. **kab tak rehenge?**   **ham das din rehenge.**
   How long will you stay?   *We'll stay for ten days.*

8. **India kaise lagta hay?**   **achchhaa lagta hay.**
   How do you like India?   *We like it.*

   or: **hinduusthaani log kaise**   **hinduusthaani log**
   lagta hay?   **achchha lagta hay.**
   How do you like Indian   *We like Indian people.*
   people?

9. **aapkaa dharm kya hay?**   **ham christian hay.**
   What's your religion?   *I'm a Christian.*

   or: **aapkii jaati kya hay?**   **ham christian hay**
   What's your caste?   *I'm a Christian.*

Note that **dharm** = *religion,* **jaati** = *caste,* but the same answer is given. It's probably the best, and certainly the easiest answer. (The 'proper' Hindi word for *Christian* is **isai**.) You could reply to the **'jaati'** question:

England me#, koi jaati nahii#.
There are no castes in England.
('England in any castes aren't'.)

But is this true? The word **jaati** could here be translated as 'social group', and you'd have to be very naive to imagine that all the different groups in England intermarried and were as one.

Again, you could reply to the **'dharm'** question:

hamaara koi dharm nahii#.
I have no religion./I don't believe in God.
('My any faith not'.)

However, this is likely to make people think you're completely mad (or possibly evil). They will happily accept whatever faith you have, but to say you have none at all is incomprehensible to the average Indian villager. Also, it is arguable that 'English' people who are atheist should still be classified as Christians, since they are a product of that culture in terms of diet, marriage and so on; they are certainly not Hindus.

10. **aap kyaa kaam karte hay?** **ham secretary hay.**
    What job do you do? *I'm a secretary.*

                                      or: **ham office me#**
                                          kaam karte hay.
                                          I work in an office.

Occupations are usually best described in English. Note that a female teacher is known as an 'eschool teacher', while a man is an 'eschool master' (not 'teacher'). In addition, remember that the verb ending changes to **-i** when spoken by/to a woman.

11. **(ek mahiine me#) kitna**   tiis hazaar rupeyaa.
     paise milta hay?   *30,000 rupees (in one month).*
     How much do you earn?

Note that if you simply quote your wage in rupees, this
will give the impression that we Western visitors are much
richer than we actually are – and that is embarrassing
enough. So, it's worth trying to give some background
information about the cost of living back home. The
examples that follow are notional; the exchange rate of 50
rupees to £1 could be changed at the stroke of a pen, and
whether you alter the amounts seen below to reflect more
accurately your own circumstances is your choice.

ek mahiine me# tiis hazaar rupeya milta.
I earn 30,000 rupees a month.

lekin isse daas hazaar rupeya tax hay.
From this, 10,000 is tax.

aur kamra kaa kiraya paa#nch hazaar rupeya hay.
Rent is 5,000.

khaana ke lie paa#nch hazaar rupeya chaahiye.
You need 5,000 for food.

England me# sab chiiz mahangi hay.
All things are expensive in the UK.
(**sab** = *all,* **chiiz** = *things,* and sounds like 'cheese',
mahangi = *expensive.*)

ek chaay kamsekam daas rupeyaa hay.
A tea is at least ten rupees.

ek meal kamsekam ek sau rupeya.
A meal is at least 100 rupees.

This will inevitably provoke cries of horror, **baap re baap!** In
fact, some people will want to hear about the prices in your
unbelievably expensive country for hours upon end. You
might be asked either:

gaariib log kyaa karna?
What do poor people do?

or: **kyaa England me# gaariib log hay?**
Are there poor people in England?

A very good question. The answer would be 'No' from an Indian perspective, but 'Yes' from an English one.

12. This question depends on whether you're alone or not. If you are alone, expect:

(kyaa) aap akela hay?	**jii haa#, ham akela hay.**
Are you alone?	*Yes sir, I'm alone.*
or: **aapke saath koi nahii#?**	**jii haa#, hamaare saath**
Isn't anybody with you?	**koi nahii#.**
	No, nobody's with me.

If you are not alone:

aapkaa saathi kaun hay?	**yeh mera dost hay.**
Who's your companion?	*This is my friend.*
or: **aapke saath kaun hay?**	**yeh mera dost hay.**
Who's with you?	*This is my friend.*
or: **yeh kaun hay?**	**yeh meri biibiijii hay**
Who is this?	*This is my wife.*

saathi = *companion*, **dost** = *friend* (it rhymes with 'toast', rather than 'lost'), **kaun?** = *who?/which?*, **biibiijii** = *(lady) wife*, **koi** = *anybody*, **aapke saath** = *with you*. You should also notice that **saathi** is a noun whereas **saath** is a preposition, like **se**.

Describing relationships to Indian people can be tricky because there is no word to describe a friendship between a man and a woman, and also because a woman may be considered immoral if she has a sexual relationship with a man to whom she isn't married.

A man describes his male friend as **dost**, and usually a woman describes her female friend as **sehiili**. For example:

yeh kaun hay? **yeh mera dost hay.**
Who is this? *This is my friend.* (m. + m.)
yeh meri sehiili hay.
This is my friend. (f. + f.)

If you're a man travelling with your girlfriend, it's definitely wise to say that you're married and to describe her as your wife: **meri biibiijii**. A husband is **maalik** (literally, 'master'). In pure Hindi, the words for 'wife' and 'husband' are **patni** and **pati** respectively. If you describe her as your **dost,** she will be considered loose, and you may well be asked:

achchhaa? aapki dost hay? ho sakta hay meri dost bhii hay.
Really? Your friend? Is can be my friend also? (literally).

In other words, 'if she sleeps with you maybe she'll sleep with me too' … which is obviously not what you want. (Some people say, with a twinkle in their eye, **'dost ki dostii?'** *'Friend or little friend?'* i.e. lover.)

If you wish to describe a platonic friendship with a woman, you should do it in an Indian way. Good Indian men are supposed to regard all women (except their wives) as a sister or a mother:

yeh meri behn hay. *This is my sister.* Or, better:
yeh vaise meri diidii hay. *She's like a big sister to me.*

(The word **vaise,** meaning *in that way,* comes from **kaise?** *in what way/how?*)

If people ask **kyaa England me# free sex hay?** (*Is there free sex in England?*), you should probably reply **'are bhaii, yeh gandi baat hay!!** *That is disgusting talk,* i.e. *'Of course not!'* (literally 'Oi brother, this filthy thing is'). This is much easier than trying to explain exactly how free our sex is – which is a futile conversation.

13. **shaadi kiya?**   **haa# kiya./nahii# kiya.**
    Married?   *Yes, married./Not married.*

You might be asked:
aap shaadi-shuuda hay? haa#, ham shaadi-shuuda hay.
Are you married? Yes, I'm married.

(Here, **shuuda** is a meaningless rhyming word.)

If your answer is 'yes', the next question may be:
aapkaa koi bachche hay? *Do you have any kids?*
haa#(jii), mere do bachche hay *I have two children.*
ek laRkaa aur ek laRkii *One boy and one girl.*

For other variations, refer back to Structure note 6.1.

If you answer 'no' to being married, you'll be asked:
kyo# nahii# *Why not?*

14. **aapke koi bhaai-**   **haa# ek bhaai aur**
    behn hay?   **ek behn hay.**
    Have you any brothers   *Yes, one brother and*
    or sisters?   *one sister.*

See Chapter 6 for a revision of this.

15. **maa#-baap THiik hay?**   **haa# THiik hay.**
    (or: **maataa-pitaajii**)   *Yes, they're fine.*
    Are your mum and dad OK?

Joint male/female subjects take the masculine ending.

16. **aapkaa naam kyaa hay?**   **mera naam XXX hay.**
    What is your name?   *My name is XXX.*

It is popular in Hindi to change the word order, like this:
naam kyaa hay aapkaa? naam XXX hay mera.

Another variation of the same question is:
aapkaa shubh naam kyaa hay? *What is your good name?*

Get to know India!

Culture, customs and special words

There are plenty of books which deal with the fascinating culture and customs of India, and this simple language guide is not the place for such detail. But it may help you to know the meaning of some Hindi words which are peculiar to the Hindu religion or are linked in some way to Hindu philosophy, as well as the names of the main characters.

The Hindu gods are Brahma (the creator), Vishnu (the preserver) and Shiva (the destroyer). Collectively, these gods are known as **om** – pronounced 'a-u-om', the sound of the all-pervasive universal power. All the other gods, and everything else, are manifestations of this force. Each member of the trinity has symbols of power and a wife: Brahma's wife is Sarasvati; Shiva's is Sati or Parvati; and Vishnu's is Lakhsmi. (The latter's name can be spelt in a variety of ways: you'll see Lakhsmi, Laksmi, Lakshmi.)

Shiva is recognisable by his **jutta** (dreadlocks) and **trishal** (trident), and the **naag** (cobra) around his neck. He carries a conch shell, is often a blue colour, and is seen meditating on Mount Kailash and dancing (when he is called Nataraj, the King of Dance). Shiva also has female incarnations, one of whom is the bloodthirsty Kali. She has a necklace of human skulls, four arms with weapons in each hand, matted hair and a protruding tongue, and gave her name to Calcutta. Shiva's son is Ganesh, who has an elephant's head.

Sarasvati is the goddess of learning and culture, and carries a **vinod** (a kind of violin). Lakhsmi always has coins shooting out of her hands since she's the goddess of wealth; an auto-rickshaw waalaa worships his rickshaw as Lakhsmi since it provides his livelihood. Lakhsmi is also the goddess of beauty and pleasure. Brahma is worshipped only in

Pushkar, Rajasthan; few temples are dedicated to the Creator. Vishnu is worshipped as Krishna or Rama, not as himself.

Krishna is the favourite god in the pantheon, and is seen in a variety of guises, for example: with a flute, enchanting the cowgirls; as a baby eating ghee; with a **chakra** (a discus with which he beheads his enemies). Rama and his wife Sita are considered the perfect examples of a man and a woman.

Hanuman, son of Vayu (god of the winds), is a monkey-faced god who helped Rama rescue Sita when she was abducted by Ravana, and who is often shown flying through the air with a mountain casually held in one hand. On the mountain are various plants, one of which is needed to save Rama's son Lakhsman, who is dying from a poisoned arrow. Hanuman wasn't sure which plant was the cure, so he brought the whole mountain.

A **mandir** is a temple, and a **dharamsaalaa** is a lodging-house for pilgrims. The word for 'worship' is **puja**, so an officiating priest is a **pujaarii.** The opportunity of seeing a holy person (a **guru**), a shrine or the image of a deity is known as a **darshan**; the guru himself is referred to as **gurujii** – with the respectful **jii** ending. The word for 'holy' or 'auspicious' is **shrii**, so in calling a married Hindu man or woman **shriimaan** or **shriimatii** respectively, the 'Mr' or 'Mrs' title is given added status. A **brahmin** is a priest who belongs to the highest caste or order; other caste persons are the **kshritryaa** ('warrior'), **vaishvaa** ('merchant') and **sudraa** ('servant'). The 'untouchables' are **harijan,** also called by ruder names, such as **achhuut log, bhangii** and **chandal.**

During your travels you'll probably meet the **sadhus,** ascetics or wandering monks. They have taken **sanyas**, a vow of renouncing the world (hence they are also called **sannyasi**), and there are many different sects:

• **siitaa raam baabaas,** who worship Rama and wear white.

• **shankar achaariya baabaas,** who wear saffron, cover their shaved heads and don't take drugs.

Both these sects follow Vishnu and worship him in his Krishna/Rama incarnations; they chant **'hare krisna, hare raam'**. The sects below follow Lord Shiva, chanting **'(hare) om namah shivay'** – 'Salutations to Shiva'.

- **naath baabaas,** who wear huge round earrings and usually have short hair.

- **naagaa baabaas,** the naked sadhus, who cover themselves in ash and are bad-tempered.

- **agori baabaas,** who wear black, and supposedly eat corpses!

- **bhoole babaas,** who have dreadlocks, wear red/saffron, may carry a trident, and who smoke dope.

All should be addressed as **baabaajii**. Sadhus are believed to have magical powers, and villagers often think that by saying a mantra, a line of Sanskrit 'poetry' or a religious chant, sadhus can curse or bless them.

In Hindu philosophy there are considered to have been four 'ages' (**yug**): the golden, silver, iron and now the black age. Mankind has steadily worsened in character through these ages, his goodness is decreasing. So when there's a problem in life, people will say **'aaj to kaalaa yug hay'** (*Things are bad these days*, literally 'today is so the dark age').

Lastly, a word or two of warning. Doubtless you'll visit mosques, temples and other places associated with worship. If you go on a **yatra**, a pilgrimage, and are offered **prasad** (holy food), you must take it in your right hand and you must eat it. Photography is forbidden unless you have official permission. Before entering places of worship, remember to remove your shoes. Wearing or carrying anything made of leather into a temple is frowned upon, and don't expose too much naked skin.

As far as general photography is concerned, it is always courteous to ask if your subject has any objections to being photographed. You can say **photi THiikhay?** (*is a photo ok?*).

Grammar

Prepositions

Because the Hindi equivalents of *in, on, by, from*, etc come after a noun or pronoun (the object of the sentence), they ought really to be called 'postpositions'. But why break the habit of a lifetime? Below is a list of the most common ones, including **kaa** *(of)*, which agrees in number and gender, and some compounds made from it:

ne	by
ko	to, at
me#	in
se	from, by
par	at, on
ke liye	for, for the sake of
kaa/ke/kii	of
(se) pahle	before (in time)
(ke) baad	after (in time)
(ke) saath	with
(ke) andar	inside
(ke) baahar	outside
(ke) niiche	under
(ke) piichhe	behind
(ke) saamne	in front of
(ke) biich	between
(ke) paas	near

It is important to note that a Hindi noun, pronoun or adjective changes its shape when followed by a preposition, becoming what is called the 'oblique' form. The original version is known as the 'direct' form. In some cases, there is no difference between the two forms. See the following examples:

99

My brother = **meraa bhaaii** (direct form)
From my brother = **mere bhaaii se** (oblique form)
My brothers = **mere bhaaii** (direct)
From my brothers = **mere bhaaii# se** (oblique)

Pronouns

Personal pronouns

The personal (subject) pronouns *I, you, he, she, it, we, they,* which are used when you say things like "She dances" or "We are hungry", are as follows (the pronunciation is given here, but will not be elsewhere in this section):

English	Hindi	Pronunciation	
I	**may#**	like 'may' but nasalised	
you	**tuu**	like 'too'	[Note 1]
he/she/it	**yeh**	rhymes with 'say'	[Note 2]
he/she/it	**voh**	like 'woe'	[Note 2]
we (I)	**ham**	like 'ham'	[Note 4]
you	**tum**	like 'tum'	[Note 1]
they	**ye**	rhymes with 'say'	[Note 3]
they (s/he)	**ve**	like 'weigh'	[Note 3]
you	**aap**	rhymes with 'slap'	[Note 1]

Note 1: tuu, tum and **aap** all mean *you*, but show different levels of politeness. The most informal, **tuu**, is used for children and, traditionally, enemies; **tum** is for servants and intimate friends; **aap** is the most polite (and the most useful), and a student should initially use only this form.

Note 2: yeh and **voh** seem confusing at first because they both mean *he/she/it*; **yeh** also means *this*, and **voh** *that*. The pronoun **yeh** refers to a *he/she/it* who is present at the conversation, whereas **voh** refers to a *he/she/it* who is not present. For example, if in India you are asked about your brother who is in England, you would refer to him as '**voh**'; while if he is with you during the conversation you would refer to him as **'yeh'**. Think of **yeh** as meaning *this man/ woman/thing*, and **voh** as *that man/woman/thing*. You can only tell if **yeh** or **voh** refers to a man or woman by the verb ending: **-a** (or **-e**) for men, and **-ii** for women.

Note 3: Just as Hindi has several forms of 'you' to show respect, so **ye** and **ve** are more polite versions of **yeh** and **voh.** Both **ye** and **ve** mean *they*, and also an honorific *he/she*. For example, you would refer to an absent younger brother as **'voh'**, but to an absent father as **'ve'**. (If they are present, they'd be referred to as **'yeh'** and **'ye'** respectively; both words are pronounced the same.)

Note 4: Although **may#** is the 'correct' word for *I*, it is very common for **ham** (correctly, *we*) to be used instead.

Since **ham, aap** and **ye/ve** have the same endings in all tenses, you need learn only this one form. Remember that if the subject is mixed gender (e.g. a married woman saying 'we'), the masculine form is always used.

Object pronouns

Object pronouns, used when saying things like "Where did you meet them?" ('them' being the object of the sentence), are given below. Refer to the list of subject pronouns for relative levels of politeness:

me	**mujh(ko)** or **mujhe**
you (= **tuu**)	**tujh(ko)** or **tujhe**
him/her (= **yeh**) *	**is(ko)** or **ise**
him/her (= **voh**) **	**us(ko)** or **use**
us	**ham(ko)** or **hame#**
you (= **tum**)	**tum(ko)** or **tumhe#**
them (= **ye**) *	**in(ko)** or **inhe#**
them (= **ve**) **	**un(ko)** or **unhe#**
you (= **aap**)	**aap(ko)**

* These forms are used when the person is present.
** These are used when the person is further away.

Possessive pronouns

Sometimes called possessive adjectives, possessive pronouns in English are *my, your, his, ours*, etc. The Hindi equivalents are given below. Notice that they agree in both gender and number with the noun to which they refer; the endings are **-aa** (masc. sing.), **-e** (masc. pl.), **-ii** (fem. sing. and pl.):

my	**meraa**	**mere**	**merii**
his/her	**uskaa**	**uske**	**uskii**
	iskaa*	**iske**	**iskii**
our	**hamaaraa**	**hamaare**	**hamaarii**
your	**tumhaaraa****	**tumhaare**	**tumhaarii**
your	**aapkaa****	**aapke**	**aapkii**
their	**unkaa**	**unke**	**unkii**
	inkaa*	**inke**	**inkii**

* The alternative forms **iskaa**, etc/**inkaa**, etc are from the **yeh/ye** forms (see Notes 2 and 3 above).

** The distinctions regarding **tum** and **aap** are the same as between the personal pronouns. There is a set for the least polite form **(teraa/tere/terii)**, but you needn't bother about these.

There's another possessive word, **apnaa**, which is used instead of any of these pronouns when the possessor is the subject of the sentence. It is equivalent to 'own' in English. Like the other pronouns, it agrees in both gender and number with the thing owned: **apnaa/apne/apnii**, as in the following example:

voh apnii rotii bechtaa hay.
He sells his (own) bread.

As you might imagine, the Hindi for 'of', or the apostrophe 's' ('s) – the possessive case indicator – also has to match its noun's gender and number; the thing that is possessed regulates this agreement: **kaa/ke/kii**.

Relative pronouns

Relative pronouns (*who, whom, which,* etc) are rendered by **jo:**
laRkaa jo yahaa# thaa, *the boy who was here.*

But **jo** becomes **jis** (sing.) or **jinho#** (pl.) when it is followed
by **ne** (*by*), and **jis** (sing.) or **jin** (pl.) when it is followed by
ko (*to*); see Prepositions. For example:

kuttaa jis ne billii ko maar daalaa
The dog which killed the cat.
aadmii jis ko may# ne bulaayaa
The man whom I called.

If **ko** is omitted, **jo** remains unchanged.

Nouns and adjectives

Articles

As you'll have discovered, there are no real equivalents in
Hindi to the English *a, an* or *the.*

Gender

You have to remember that every Hindi noun is either
masculine or feminine, as in French, for example. There's no
determining rule, other than that (usually) male creatures
are masculine and female ones feminine. Abstract ideas,
inanimate objects, places and so on could be either gender
(and there's no neuter). You'll just have to learn which is
which when you first come across the noun in question. As
a guideline, the names of most things are masculine (as are
the majority of nouns ending in **-aa**); nouns that end in
-ii or **-t** are usually feminine. You learn this, then discover,
for example, that **kitab** (*book*) is feminine. So be careful!

Plural forms

Masculine nouns usually remain unchanged in the plural, but those ending in **-aa** (sing.) become **-e**: **kamraa** (*room*), **kamre** (*rooms*). Singular feminine nouns ending in **-ii** change to **-iaa#**, while those ending in any other letter generally ad **-e#**. There are other plural endings, too.

Oblique forms

As mentioned earlier, nouns, adjectives and pronouns have so-called oblique forms when followed by a preposition (which, as you know, comes after the word it relates to.) These spelling modifications will not have much bearing on your street Hindi, but if you ever get around to learning the 'proper' language, they will be very much in evidence.

Adjectives: gender and number

Adjectives in Hindi often work like French adjectives; they take the same number and gender as the noun they qualify. Any adjective that doesn't end in **-aa**, and any adjective that ends in a consonant, never changes and never has an oblique form. Those that do, change only in their masculine singular and plural forms; the feminine forms remain unaltered. For example:

kharaab laRkaa *a bad boy*
kharaab laRkii *a bad girl*
but
achchhaa laRkaa *a good boy*
achchhii laRkii *a good girl*

Adjectives which do end in **-aa** (i.e. most of them) change as follows:

- With a masculine noun, **-aa** becomes **-e** in the plural, when in the subject or object case.

- With a feminine noun, the adjective ends in **-ii** in all cases and numbers.

Remember that words such as **meraa** (*my*) and **aapkaa** (*your*) are possessive adjectives, and therefore they should follow these rules.

Questions

If most of the English question words begin with a 'w' (e.g. *who, what, when, where, why, which*), then the corresponding Hindi words begin with a 'k'. This doesn't indicate anything in particular, but it may help you recall the right word at the right time!

kahaa#?	where?
kaun? *	who? which?
kyaa? *	what?
kab?	when?
kyoo#?	why?
kis?	who? which?
kaisaa?*	how? (= in what manner?)
kitnaa?*	how much? how many?

* These words change their form like other pronouns and adjectives.

The following 'time' expressions are often loosely used, without too much regard for the actual period of time involved:

kab tak?	how long? (= future, long period)
kitne din?	how long? (literally 'how many days')
kitne ghunTe?	how long? (literally, 'how many hours')

Interrogation can also be expressed by tone of voice, emphasizing the last word of the sentence:

Tum nahii# jaante? *Don't you know?*

Verbs

a) *I am, he is, you are …*

The Hindi verb **honaa** (*to be*) is the only one that can be said to have 'proper' present and past tenses, and you have used it a lot in your street Hindi – remember **hay**, which crops up in numerous dialogues? Below is a more formal showing of the entire present tense:

I am	**may# huu#**
you are	**tuu hay** (the very familiar form)
he/she/it is	**yeh hay, voh hay**
we are	**ham hay#**
you are (pl.)	**tum ho** (familiar)
they are *	**ye hay#, ve hay#**
you are	**aap hay#**

* also 'these/those are'

b) *I was, he was, you were …*

Here is the past tense. Notice the feminine forms.

	masculine	*feminine*
I was	**may# thaa**	**may# thii**
you were	**tuu thaa**	**tuu thii**
he/she/it was	**yeh thaa, voh thaa**	**yeh thii, voh thii**
we were	**ham the**	**ham thii#**
you were (pl.)	**tum the**	**tum thii#**
they were*	**ye the, ve the**	**ye thii#, ve thii#**
you were	**aap the**	**aap thii#**

* also *these/those were*

Verb patterns

Remind yourself of the personal pronouns listed earlier and then study the following verb patterns. These show the full, correct usage of verbs; up to now, in our street Hindi, you've covered the two most commonly used parts (**aap** and **ham**), but the whole picture is necessary if you want to speak more formally.

All verbs in Hindi have a stem (the front part) which is unchangeable, and an ending, which changes according to the tense as well as the gender/number/status of the subject:

denaa	to give
ye dete hay	he gives
ye detii hay	she gives
ye denge	he will give

So the stem is '**de**'.

Present simple

The straightforward present tense is formed by the verb stem + **-te** (male subject) or **-tii** (female subject) + **hay**, in the most useful **aap/ham/ye** form. As an example, look at **jaanaa** (*to go*); the stem is **jaa**:

male	*female*	
may# jaataa huu#	**may# jaatii huu#**	I go
tuu jaataa hay	**tuu jaatii hay**	you go
yeh/voh jaataa hay	**yeh/voh jaatii hay**	he/she/it goes
ham jaate hay#	**ham jaatii hay#**	we go
tum jaate ho	**tum jaatii ho**	you go
ye/ve jaate hay#	**ye/ve jaatii hay#**	they go
aap jaate hay#	**aap jaatii hay#**	you go

In proper Hindi, **hay** becomes nasalised (**hay#**) for use with **aap/ham/ye**. In 'street' Hindi this is usually ignored, so don't worry about it.

Present continuous

This version of the present tense (*I am going, you are going,* etc) is formed by the stem + **-rehe** (men) or **-rehi** (women) + **hay**, in the **aap/ham/ye** form. (Note that the 'eh' in **reha/ rehi** is almost silent, so pronounce **reha** as 'ra', **rehe** as 're', **rehii** as 'rii'.)

As an example, look at **aanaa** (to come); the stem is **aa-**:

male	*female*	
may# aa reha huu#	**may# aa rehii huu#**	I am coming
tuu aa reha hay	**tuu aa rehii hay**	you are coming
yeh/voh aa reha hay	**yeh/voh aa rehii hay**	he/etc is coming
ham aa rehe hay	**ham aa rehii hay#**	we are coming
tum aa rehe ho	**tum aa rehii ho**	you are coming
ye/ve aa rehe hay#	**ye/ve aa rehii hay#**	they are coming
aap aa rehe hay#	**ap aa rehii hay#**	you are coming

Subjunctive

The subjunctive (*I may look, we may look,* etc) is formed by the stem + **-e#** in **aap/ham/ye** forms. There is no difference between the masculine and feminine forms.

For example, **dekhnaa** (*to look at, to see*), the stem of which is **dekh-**:

male and *female*	
may# dekhuu#	I may see
tuu dekhe	you may see
yeh/voh dekhe	he/she/it may see
ham dekhe#	we may see
tum dekho	you may see
ye/ve dekhe#	they may see
aap dekhe#	you may see

The subjunctive is not used very often – except the **'tum'** form as a command – but it is included here because it makes up part of the future tense.

Future

The future tense is formed by adding **-ga/-ge** (men) or **-gii** (women) to the subjunctive. The nasalised plural/polite forms are written '**n**' instead of '**#**' for convenience; you could say or write either **khaae#ge** or **khaaenge**.

The model verb is **khaanaa** (*to eat*); its stem is **khaa-**:

male	*female*	
may# khaaunga	**may# khaauungii**	I will eat
tuu khaaega	**tuu khaaegii**	you will eat
yeh/voh khaaega	**yeh/voh khaaegii**	he/she/it will eat
ham khaaenge	**ham khaaengii**	we will eat
tum khaaoge	**tum khaaogii**	you will eat
ye/ve khaaenge	**ye/ve khaaenge**	they will eat
aap khaaenge	**aap khaaenge**	you will eat

Past

The past tense is formed by putting the subject + **ne (which doesn't mean anything but shows which word is the subject)** + the object + stem of the verb + **-aa/-e/-ii** (which agrees in gender with the object). For example:

ham ne kela khaaya. *We ate a banana.*
(Bananas are masculine, so it's **khaaya.**)
ham ne chapaatii khaayii. *We ate a chapati.*
(Chapatis are feminine, so it's **khaayii.**)

(Exceptionally, **aana**, *to come*, and **jaana**, *to go*, don't use **ne** and agree with the subject, i.e. they conform to the normal pattern of **-a/-e** and female **-ii** agreement.)

All things in Hindi are male or female, so to speak proper Hindi you must know their gender. There's no logic as to which is which, so you have to learn them one by one. Luckily, however, the full form of the past tense is rarely spoken. In 'street' Hindi, all objects are taken as masculine for convenience, so all past tenses end in **-a.**

Some verbs slightly change their root in the past tense; those stems ending in **-aa** add a **-y**, while those ending in **-e** change this to **-iy**, as do **karnaa** and other irregular verbs, listed here:

infinitive	English	past	pronunciation
karnaa	to do	**kiya**	'key+ah'
denaa	to give	**diya**	'dee+ah'
lenaa	to take	**liya**	'lee+ah'
piinaa	to drink/smoke	**piya**	'pee+ah'
aanaa	to come	**aaya/aaye** [m.]	'eye+ah'/ 'eye+eh'
		aayii [f.]	'eye+eee'
jaanaa	to go	**gaya/gaye** [m.]	'guy+ah'/ 'guy+eh'
		gayii [f.]	'guy+eee'
laanaa	to bring	**laaya**	'lie+ah'
khaanaa	to eat	**khaaya**	'kye+ah'

Note the male [m.] and female [f.] forms for **aanaa** and **jaanaa** – and that **jaanaa** changes from **j** to **g**. For example:

Indira Gandhi Delhi gayii. *Indira Gandhi went to Delhi.*
Mahatma Gandhi Delhi gaye. *Mahatma Gandhi went to Delhi.*

Some past tense forms of regular verbs are:

dekhnaa *(to see)*	**dekha**
milnaa *(to meet)*	**mila**
bolnaa *(to say, speak)*	**bola**
sunnaa *(to hear)*	**suna**

When making a (correct) Hindi past tense sentence, you need: (1) subject (2) **ne** (3) object (4) verb. As follows: (1) **aap** (2) **ne** (3) **India** (4) **dekha**

Note that the pronouns **yeh/voh** change to **is/us**, and **ye/ve** become **in/un**, when followed by **ne**. For example: **un ne kebab khaaya.** *He ate a kebab.*

In Hindi, especially informal Hindi, the pronoun subject is often omitted; the context and verb ending make it clear who or what the subject is. Thus, a tourist will always be asked **'shaadi kiya?'** (*'Are you married?'*), which is short for **'kyaa aap ne shaadi kiya?'** (literally 'You marriage made'). In fact, **shaadi** is feminine, so **kiya** should be **kiyi** to agree; but you're unlikely to hear this version since the Indians who speak correct (or formal) Hindi are more likely also to speak English, which they'll use when talking to you.

Commands and polite requests

These forms convey several meanings, from the polite 'Would you please sit down' to the impolite 'Sit!'. You'll hear children addressed in the **tuu** form, shopkeepers in the **aap** form, and customers in the most polite 'super'-**aap** (**+aap**) form. Listen to conversations, and you can work out the status of the participants. Here's a table of these four modes of address:

		construction	*example*
tuu	bare root	**dekh!**	Look!
tum	root + **o**	**dekho!**	Look (friend)!
aap	root + **na**	**dekhna**	Look, please.
+aap	root + **iye**	**dekhiye***	Please, would you look

* **-iye** sounds like the letters 'E.A.'.

Verbs whose roots end in **-aa** make the sound 'ow' (as in 'how') when an **o** is added. For example: **jaao** is like 'jow(l)'; **aao** is (pretty clearly) like 'ow!'; and **khaao** is like 'cow'. The **-na** form (e.g. **dena**) can mean either *to go, going* or *please go*. The context will show which.

Some verbs change in the **-iye** form:

dena becomes **didgiye**
piina becomes **pidgiye**   } pronounced to rhyme
lena becomes **lidgiye**   with 'midge' + E.A.
karna becomes **kidgiye**

In the **tum** form, **dena** and **lena** lose their **-e-** to become **do** and **lo** (not **deo** and **leo**).

Passive voice

The passive form (*it was eaten, Hindi is spoken,* etc) consists of the past tense of the main verb + the correct tense of **jaanaa**, both of which (should) agree in gender with that of the object (NOT the subject). For example: **UP meE hindi bolii jaatii hai**: *Hindi is spoken in Uttar Pradesh.*

A simplified verb chart

Here is the **ham/aap/ye** form of the most useful tenses of the most useful verbs. Note the abbreviated endings, and remember that **-e** is for men, or men and women together, and that **-ii** is for women only. Repeat them using the correct ending for your own gender.

infin.	*pres. simple*	*pres. contin.*	*future*	*past*
jaanaa	jaate hay	jaa rehe hay	jaaenge	gaye
to go	jaatii hay	jaa rehii hay	jaaengii	gayii
aanaa	aate/ii hay	aa rehe/ii hay	aaenge/ii	aaye/ii
to come				
lenaa	lete/ii hay	le rehe/ii hay	lenge/ii	liya
to take				
denaa	dete/ii hay	de rehe/ii hay	denge/ii	diya
to give				
piinaa	piite/ii hay	pii rehe/ii hay	piienge/ii	piya
to drink/smoke				
karnaa	karte/ii hay	kar rehe/ii hay	karenge/ii	kiya
to do/make				
laanaa	laate/ii hay	laa rehe/ii hay	laaenge/ii	laaya
to bring				
rehnaa	rehte/ii hay	reh rehe/ii hay	rehenge/ii	reha
to live/stay				
khaanaa	khaate/ii hay	khaa rehe/ii hay	khaaenge/ii	khaaya
to eat				
dekhnaa	dekhte/ii hay	dekh rehe/ii hay	dekhenge/ii	dekha
to see/look at				
sunnaa	sunte/ii hay	sun rehe/ii hay	sunenge/ii	suna
to listen to				

Here are the same verbs in their command forms.
Remember, the **aap** form is the safest and easiest to use.

	tuu	tum	aap	'super'-**aap**
	form	*form*	*form*	*form*
jaanaa	jaa	jaao	jaana	jaaiye
aanaa	aa	aao	aana	aaiye
lenaa	le	lo	lena	lidgiye
denaa	de	do	dena	didgiye
piinaa	pii	piio	piina	pidgiye
karnaa	kar	karo	karna	kidgiye
laanaa	laa	laao	laana	laaiye
rehnaa	reh	reho	rehna	rehiy
khaanaa	khaa	khaao	khaana	khaaiye
dekhnaa	dekh	dekha	dekhna	dekhiye
sunnaa	sun	suna	sunna	suniye

Compound verbs

In Hindi it is very common to use a second verb tacked on
to the first, without changing the meaning. (In fact, the second verb can change the shade of meaning, but for now we
will look only at those verbs which don't.) This might seem
a strange system, but in fact it is very easy to understand –
as well as being important to learn. Indians use it all the time.

You use the stem of the first (main) verb and the appropriate tense of the second (meaningless) verb. Most of the time,
lenaa, jaanaa and **denaa** are the compound verbs used. The
most common of these is **lenaa**, which is often added to **dekh,
siikh, ghuum, pii, kaa**. Normally, **lenaa** means *to take,* but in
compound uses it doesn't have any meaning (though it
sometimes suggests conscious effort). Look at the following
examples:

(i) **dekh lenaa** = **dekhna** *to look at*
     ham Agra dekh lenge. = **ham Agra dekhenge.**
     We'll see Agra.
     ham Taaj Mahaal dekh liya. = **ham Taaj Mahaal dekha.**
     We've seen the Taj Mahal.

113

(ii) **siikh lenaa** = **siikhna** *to learn*
      ham Madras me# tamil siikh lenge. = ... **tamil siikhenge**
      We'll learn Tamil in Madras.
      aap hindi kahaa# siikh liya? = **aap hindi kahaa# siikha?**
      Where did you learn Hindi?

(iii) **ghuum lenaa** = **ghuumna** *to wander*
      aap India me# kahaa# ghuum lenge? = ... **ghuumenge**
      Where will you wander/travel in India?
      Delhi (me#) ghuum liya? = **Delhi (me#) ghuuma?**
      Have you been around Delhi?

(iv) **pii lenaa** = **piina** *to drink, to smoke*
     chaay pii liya? = **chaay piya?**
     Have you drunk your tea?
     nahii# ham baad me# chaay pii lenge. = ... **chaay piienge.**
     No, we'll drink tea afterwards.

baad me# (literally, 'afterwards in' – the **me#** is necessary in
Hindi) is a handy way of refusing invitations: when a street
trader says "Hello, you like carpet?", you can say **baad me#,
bhaaii** (*Later, mate*). If you want to say "After Delhi we'll go
to Agra", the construction is different: **Delhi ke baad ham
Agra jaaenge** (literally, 'Delhi of after we Agra will go').

(v) **khaa lenaa** = **khaana** *to eat*
     khaana khaa liya? = **khaana khaaya?**
     Have you eaten?
     nahii# baad me# khaana khaa lenge = ... **khaana
     khaaenge.**
     No, we'll eat later.

khaana = *a meal* (noun), **khaana** = *to eat a meal* (verb). So
khaana khaana is *to eat a main meal*. The two words can also
be used separately:

khaana kitna hay? *How much are meals?*
samosa khaa liya? *Have you eaten the samosa?*

The main point to remember here is that the **'lenaa'** in **dekh
lena, khaa lenaa,** etc has no meaning. While you must be

able to recognise these compounds, you can always use the simple constructions – **piienge** instead of **pii lenge**. However, the compound construction is so easy (once you've got the hang of it) that you really should use it. This is how Indians speak – and without compound verbs your Hindi will sound unnatural.

(vi) **jaanaa**: as a compound verb it suggests completeness:
   baiTHo: sit! – **baiTH jaao!** Sit yourself down.
   sonaa: to sleep – **soojaao!** Go to sleep.

It is often used with **hona** (to be). **ho jaanaa** (to become). For example: **chaay THanDaa ho jaaegaa:** the tea will become cold.

(vii) **denaa:** as a compound verb it suggests emphasis. Like **lenaa**, it is commonly used with itself. For example:

ek chaay do: *give us tea*
ek chaay de do! *do give us tea*
ek chaay banaao: *make us tea*
ek chaay banaa do: *do make us tea*

Special compound verbs

There are certain very common verbs which tack on to the main verb and which do have a special meaning:

(i) **rehna** *to remain*
   Put the past tense (i.e. **rehe/rehii** + **hay**) after the stem of the main verb, to make the equivalent of the English '-ing' as used in the present continuous tense. This is extremely common. For example:

ham sigret pii rehe hay. *I'm* [m.] *smoking a ciggie.*
ham aa rehii hay. *I'm* [f.] *coming.*

When spoken, the verbs are really squashed together so that **rehe** becomes **re**, and **rehii** becomes **rii**. Thus, **pii rehe hay** sounds like 'piirehay', and so on.

(ii) **chuukna** *to have completed*

Put the inflected past tense + **hay** after another verb root, and this means 'to have already done something':

ham chaay pii chuuka hay. *I've* [m.] *already had a tea.*
Kashmiir jaa chuuki hay. *I've* [f.] *already been to Kashmir.*
ham de chuuka hay. *I've already given.* (Useful for beggars.)

(iii) **sakna** *to be able*

This must be used with another verb, not alone. Put the stem of the main verb, then the suitable tense (usually the present), inflected, + **hay** (optional) after the root, to make the construction 'I can/can't do ...'. For example:

jaa sakna *to be able to go*
pii sakna *to be able to smoke*
reh sakna *to be able to stay*
videshi log Nagaland nahii# jaa sakte (hay).
Foreigners can't go to Nagaland.
bhaaii, ham das rupeya nahii# de sakta.
I [m.] *can't pay ten rupees, mate.*
ham itna chaay nahii# pii saktii.
I [f.] *can't drink this much tea.*

Causative verbs

From the verbs you know already, you can make more, usually by adding **aa** before the **naa**. This changes the meaning to a causitive one, which is often translated by a completely different verb in English. For example:

chalnaa (to move) – **chalaanaa**: to drive (to make move)
ghuumnaa (to wander) – **ghuumaanaa**: to guide (to make wander
uTHnaa (to get up, to rise) – **uTHaanaa**: to lift up
thaknaa (to be tired) – **thakaanaa**: to make tired
paRHnaa (to read, study) – **paRHaanaa**: to teach (make study)

(Reciting these aloud is a good way to practise saying **a** and **aa** sounds.

The Hindi Verb Wheel

The verb wheel is a fun and easy way to help you master verbs in Hindi. Simply follow the instructions on how to make your own wheel, and then do the exercises.

Making your verb wheel

The verb wheel consists of two revolving discs mounted on a base. On the left-hand wheel are some common verb stems, and on the right are the verb endings you need to make the main tenses in Hindi. The verb wheel allows you to match up different combinations of verb stems with verb endings to provide plenty of practice with verbs. Begin by copying the diagrams on pages 120–21. Do this directly onto some plain card, or onto paper that you can then stick onto some card. Cut the two circles out, and use drawing pins or paper fasteners to attach them side-by-side onto a single base. Once they are in place, you should be able to turn the wheels to align any verb stem from the left-hand wheel with any verb ending from the right-hand wheel, at the point where the wheels meet.

Using your verb wheel

The verb wheel allows you to make the following tenses: present simple, present continuous, future and past. It also lets you make three levels of command or request.

Tenses: *go, am going, will go, went*

Practise using the future form, which consists of a verb stem from the left-hand wheel, with the appropriate endings from the right-hand wheel – **enge** or **engii** (**e** ending for men, **ii** for women). Line up **jaa** on the left-hand wheel and **enge** on the right-hand wheel to form **jaaenge**, *'will go'* (in Hindi you don't need to use 'I', 'you', 'she', 'he', 'it', 'we' or 'they'). Now, with a map of India, say all the places you would go to as if you were travelling around the country. For example: **Dehli jaaenge**, *I/we will go to Delhi*; **Bombay jaaenge**, *I/we will go to Bombay*.

Do this with ten places, then expand it with **nahii#** ('no'), e.g. **Calcutta nahii jaaenge**, *I/we will not go to Calcutta*. Rotate the left wheel one section anti-clockwise to make **laaenge**, *I/we will bring*. Practise this with 'passport', 'camera' and so on, remembering that the object always comes before the verb. Then, rotate the verb stem wheel through each section to produce the verbs below.

khaaenge	*I/we will eat*	(e.g. chapati)
bunaaenge	*I/we will make*	(e.g. tea)
lenge	*I/we will take*	(e.g. photos)
deenge	*I/we will give*	(e.g. baksheesh)
piienge	*I/we will smoke*	(e.g. cigarettes)
piienge	*I/we will drink*	(e.g. water, beer, whisky)
karenge	*I/we will do*	(e.g. trekking, yoga)
rehenge	*I/we will stay*	(e.g. **Delhi me** = in Delhi)
dekhenge	*I/we will see*	(e.g. Taj Mahal, Himalayas)
milenge	*I/we will meet*	(e.g. friends, village people)
chelenge	*I/we will move*	(e.g. **bus se** = by bus)
sunenge	*I/we will listen*	(e.g. to music)
aaenge	*I/we will come*	(e.g. **October me vapas aaenge** = we will come back in October)

Now turn the right wheel again to create a present tense ending: verb stem + **te** for men/**tii** for women + **hay** if you want (though Indians often drop it). Use the present tense to talk about daily routines using the verb stems on the left-hand wheel. e.g. **cigarette (nahii#) piite**, *I don't smoke cigarettes*.

Now practise using the present continuous – verb stem + **re** + **hay** for men, or stem + **rii** + **hay** for women – to talk about things that you are doing at the moment. For example: **biriyani khaa re hay**, *I am eating biryani*.

Now practise the past tense: stem + **aa** for both men and women (except with the verbs **aanaa** and **jaanaa**, which end in **aa** for men and **ii** for women). Note that the light shaded verbs on the left-hand wheel (with the stems **aa, jaa, laa, khaa, bunaa**) all add **y** + **aa** in the past – becoming **laayaa, khaayaa**, and so on. Note that **aanaa** ('to come') becomes **aayaa** for men, **aayii** for women, and that **jaanaa** ('to go') becomes **gaayaa** for men, **gaayii** for women (and sounds like 'guy' + a). Also note that dark-shaded verbs, with the stems **le, de, pii** and **kar**, become **liyaa, diyaa, piyaa, kiyaa**, sounding like lee + yaa, as in 'phobia'.

Commands and requests

Now turn the right-hand wheel to the **na** ending (which is the most useful) and say, for example: **coffee dena** (*please give me a coffee*). For very polite requests, turn the right-hand wheel to **iye** (pronounced like 'E.A.') and say, for example: **chapaati khaaiye** (*would you like to eat a chapati?*) Note that the dark-shaded verbs on the verb stem wheel (**le, de**, etc) change to 'lidgeEa', 'didgeEA', and so on (rhyming with midge + E.A.). You can now produce the following:

(e.g. bill)	**laaiye**	*would you please bring*
(e.g. biscuit)	**khaaiye**	*... please eat*
(e.g. tea)	**bunaaiye**	*... please make*
(e.g. money)	**lijiye**	*... please take*
(e.g. coffee)	**dijiye**	*... please give*
(e.g. cigarette)	**pijiye**	*... please smoke*
(e.g. beer)	**pijiye**	*... please drink*
(e.g. repair)	**kijiye**	*... please do*
(e.g. hotel)	**rehiye**	*... please stay*
(e.g. Taj Mahal)	**dekhiye**	*... please see*
(e.g. the car)	**cheliye**	*... please move*
(e.g. once)	**suniye**	*... please listen*

For commands for juniors, turn the right-hand wheel to **o**, e.g. **suno** (*listen*), **chelo** (*move*). Note that light-shaded verbs have the sound 'ow' (as in 'how' not 'hoe'), and that de + o becomes 'do' (like 'doe' not 'do'), and that le + o sounds like 'low'.

Verb stems

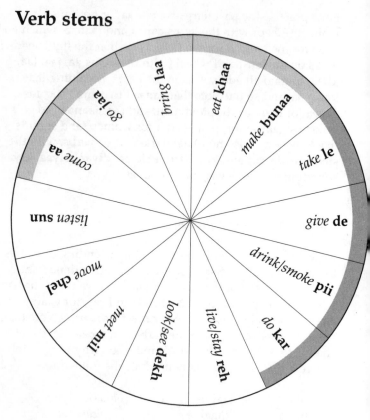

How to make the verb wheel

- *You will need: cardboard for the base and the two wheels, two drawing pins or paper fasteners, paper.*
- *Copy the diagrams above directly onto some plain card, or onto paper that you can then stick onto some card (beer mats are perfect). Use drawing pins or paper fasteners to attach them side-by-side onto a single base.*
- *If you have access to a photocopier, this may be quicker.*

Verb endings

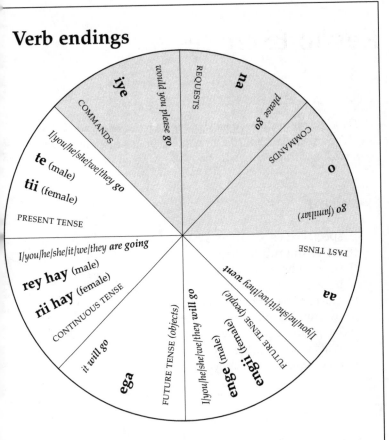

How to use the verb wheel

- *Rotate the left-hand wheel so that the verb stem you want to use is in the three o'clock position.*
- *Now match your chosen verb stem with a verb ending from the right-hand wheel: rotate the right-hand wheel so that your chosen verb ending is in the nine o'clock position.*
- *You can now read your Hindi verb at the point where the wheels meet.*

Key to Exercises

These are the answers to most of the exercises found in chapters 1–7; those to Exercise 10 are excluded; in this case refer to the preceding Structure note).

Exercise 1

b) special chaay do rupeya hay.
c) coffee tiin rupeya hay.
d) pepsi chhe rupeya hay.
e) bisleri das rupeya hay.
f) glucose biscuit chaar rupeya hay.
g) coconut biscuit paa#ch rupeya hay.
h) 7-Up saat rupeya hay.
i) Wills aaTH rupeya hay.
j) Four Square nao rupeya hay.

Exercise 2

b) *says* tiin coffee dena.
c) *says* do packet glucose biscuits dena.
d) *says* ek pepsi dena.

Exercise 3

a) yeh kyaa hay?   yeh chaawal hay.
   yeh kyaa hay?   yeh chapaatii hay.
   yeh kyaa hay?   yeh daal hay.
   yeh kyaa hay?   yeh daal fry hay.
   yeh kyaa hay?   yeh aaluu gobhii hay.
   yeh kyaa hay?   yeh aaluu matar hay.
   yeh kyaa hay?   yeh matar paniir hay.

b) yeh kitna paise hay?	yeh tiin rupeya hay.
yeh kitna paise hay?	yeh ek rupeya hay.
yeh kitna paise hay?	yeh do rupeya hay.
yeh kitna paise hay?	yeh tiin rupeya hay.
yeh kitna paise hay?	yeh chaar rupeya hay.
yeh kitna paise hay?	yeh paa#ch rupeya hay.
yeh kitna paise hay?	yeh chhe rupeya hay.

Exercise 4

b) ek matar paniir aur ek chaawal dena.
c) tiin daal aur do chaawal dena.
d) ek aaluu gobhii aur ek daal aur chaar chapaatii dena.
e) do coffee aur ek packet coconut biscuit dena.

Exercise 5

a) How much is this?
b) What is this?
c) Is this daal fry?
d) Is this three rupees?
e) Is the tea OK?
f) Yes, the tea is OK.
g) No, the tea isn't OK.

Exercise 6

1. *Each puts the same set of four questions to the others:*

a) hindi aatii hay?
b) angrezi aatii hay?
c) gujarati aatii hay?
d) punjabi aatii hay?

In the following replies, remember that the bracketed **haa# jii**
(or **jii haa#**) *and* **jii nahii#** *are optional; they simply make the
sentence more polite, without changing the meaning.*
Sonya answers Ramesh:

a) (haa# jii) kuchh kuchh.
b) (haa# jii) angrezi aatii hay.
c) (jii nahii#) kuchh nahii#.
d) (jii nahii#) punjabi nahii# aatii.

Raju answers Sonya:
a) (jii nahii#) hindi nahii# aatii.
b) (jii nahii#) kuchh nahii#.
c) (haa# jii) kuchh kuchh.
d) (haa# jii) punjabi aatii hay.

Sheila answers Raju:
a) (jii) thoRa thoRa.
b) (jii haa#) kuchh kuchh.
c) (jii haa#) gujarati aatii hay.
d) (jii haa#) thoRa kuchh.

Ramesh answers Sheila:
a) (jii haa#) hindi aatii hay.
b) (jii) thoRa thoRa.
c) (jii nahii#) gujarati nahii# aatii.
d) (jii haa#) kuchh kuchh.

2. *For example:*
hindi aatii hay? tamil aatii hay? gujarati aatii hay?

Exercise 7

a) *1 asks 3:* aap kahaa# se hay?
   Reply: ham Calcutta se hay.
   1 asks 4: aap kahaa# se hay?
   Reply: ham Bombay se hay.
   1 asks 5: aap kahaa# se hay?
   Reply: ham Bangalore se hay.
   1 asks 6: aap kahaa# se hay?
   Reply: ham Ahmadabad se hay.

b) *6 asks 1:* bengali aatii hay?
   Reply: (jii nahii#) bengali nahii# aatii.
   6 asks 1: hindi aatii hay?

Reply: (jii haa#) hindi aatii hay.
6 asks 2: tamil aatii hay?
Reply: (jii haa#) tamil aatii hay.
6 asks 2: telugu aatii hay?
Reply: kuchh kuchh/thoRa thoRa, etc.
6 asks 3: bengali aatii hay?
Reply: (jii haa#) bengali aatii hay.
6 asks 3: punjabi aatii hay?
Reply: (jii nahii#) punjabi nahii# aatii.
6 asks 4: maraathi aatii hay?
Reply: (jii haa#) maraathi aatii hay.
6 asks 4: gujarati aatii hay?
Reply: thoRa kuchh/kuchh kuchh, etc.
6 asks 5: kannada aatii hay?
Reply: (jii haa#) kannada aatii hay.
6 asks 5: tamil aatii hay?
Reply: thoRa thoRa/kuchh kuchh, etc.

Exercise 8

1 asks 2: whisky kaise lagta hay?
Reply: whisky achchhaa lagta hay.
1 asks 2: cricket kaise lagte hay?
Reply: cricket achchhaa nahii# lagta.
1 asks 2: cigarettes kaise lagte hay?
Reply: cigarettes achchhaa nahii# lagta.
1 asks 3: beer/whisky/cricket/cigarettes kaise lagte hay?
Reply: beer achchhaa nahii# lagta; whisky achch haa
             nahii# lagta; cricket achchhaa lagta hay;
             cigarettes achchhaa lagta hay.
1 asks 4: beer/whisky/cricket/cigarettes kaise lagte
             hay?
Replies: beer achchhaa nahii# lagta; whisky achch haa
             nahii# lagta; cricket achchhaa lagta hay;
             cigarettes achchhaa nahii# lagta.

In reply to the same questions, 1 replies: beer achchhaa lagta
hay; whisky achchhaa lagta hay; cricket achchhaa nahii#
lagta; cigarettes achchhaa lagta hay.

Exercise 9

Some model questions and answers:
Q: Calcutta kahaa# hay? (Where is Calcutta?)
A: Calcutta West Bengal me# hay.
Q: Kyaa Calcutta West Bengal me# hay? (Is Calcutta in West Bengal?)
A: haa#jii, Calcutta West Bengal me# hay.
Q: Kyaa Calcutta Kerala me# hay? (Is Calcutta in Kerala?)
A: jii nahii#, Calcutta Kerala me# nahii#./Calcutta West Bengal me# hay.
Q: Jaipur kahaa# hay? (Where is Jaipur?)
A: Jaipur Rajasthan me# hay.
Q: Kyaa Jaipur Gujarat me# hay? (Is Jaipur in Gujarat?)
A: jii nahii#, Jaipur Gujarat me# nahii#./Jaipur Rajasthan me# hay.
Q: Kyaa Bombay Orissa me# hay? (Is Bombay in Orissa?)
A: jii nahii#, Bombay Orissa me# nahii#.
Q: Bombay kahaa# hay? (Where is Bombay?)
A: Bombay Maharashtra me# hay.   *... and so on.*

Exercise 11

a) kyaa haal hay (diidii)? *or* THiik hay (diidii)? *or* (aap) kaisii hay?
b) achchhii baat hay!
c) koi muskil nahii#; *or* kuchh muskil nahii#; *or* koi tak lif nahii#.
d) Varanasi bhii Uttar Pradesh me# hay.
e) THiik hay (bhaaii)? *or* kyaa haal hay (bhaaii)?
f) (bas) THiik hay aur aap?
g) aafsos kii baat (hay).
h) bill THiik nahii#.

Exercise 12

a) ... sasta waala.
b) ... cotton waala.
c) ... THanDa waala.
d) ... pukka waala.
e) ... buRa waala.

Exercise 13

a) 330	g) ek sao terah.
b) 419	h) paa#ch sao pachaas.
c) 550	i) saat hazaar do sao pachchiis.
d) 120	j) chaar sao unniis.
e) 970	k) tiin sao tiis.
f) 7225	l) nao sao sattar.

Exercise 14

In this exercise, (a) is primarily an oral exercise in which you simply preface the phrase **kitne paise hay?** *with the appropriate item. (c) is also designed for oral practice and covers items 1 to 6 only. (b) needs a little more working out, and you might want to write down the prices before speaking them:*

1. aam gyaarah rupeya kaa kilo hay.
2. liichii pondrah rupeya kaa kilo hay.
3. santara aaTH rupeya kaa kilo hay.
4. muung phuli do rupeya kaa kilo hay.
5. sev aaTH rupeya kaa kilo hay.
6. anguur nao rupeya kaa kilo hay.
7. pista pondrah rupeya kaa sao gram hay.
8. baadaam aTHTHaarah rupeya kaa sao gram hay.
9. caajuu solah rupeya kaa sao gram hay.
10. khishmish chaudah rupeya kaa sao gram hay.

Exercise 15

This is another oral exercise which doesn't require all the answers here. Whether you choose to say (line 3) "Hello, have you got 1 kg of mangoes and 2 kg of apples?" or to mix items (e.g. "… 1 kg of mangoes and kg of sugar?") is entirely up to you and your expertise! Here, though, are translations of the five lines:

a) ek sao gram pista, tiin sao gram baadaam, chaar sao gram khishmish.
b) paa#ch nimbu, aadha kilo santara, ek kilo anguur.

c) ek kilo aam, do kilo sev.
d) deRH kilo liichii.
e) saaRHe tiin kilo chaawal, aadha kilo chini.

Exercise 16

1 *asks* 2:	kidher jaana?/kahaa# jaana?
Reply:	ham Delhi jaana.
2 *asks* 3:	kidher jaana?/kahaa# jaana?
Reply:	ham Kanpur jaana.
3 *asks* 4:	kidher jaana?/kahaa# jaana?
Reply:	ham Calcutta jaana.
4 *asks* 1:	kidher jaana?/kahaa# jaana?
Reply:	ham Agra jaana.

For extra practice you can also make 1 ask 3, 4 and 5 where they're going, but the questions and answers will be the same.

Exercise 17

1. subah ko sahRe chhe baje.
2. raat ko paone nao baje.
3. subah ko savva das baje.
4. tiin baje.
5. din ko chaar das.
6. subah ko sahRe nao baje.
7. raat ko baara baje.

a) midnight. b) 9.30am.   c) 4.10pm.   d) 3pm.
e) 3.00*   f) 10.15am.   g) 8.45pm.   h) 6.30am.

* am/pm unspecified.

Exercise 18

Tourist:	How much is a ticket to Delhi?
Clerk:	110 rupees.
Tourist:	I see/Really?/Yeah? One ticket, please … When will the Delhi train leave?
Clerk:	The Delhi train leaves at 6am.
Tourist:	And when does it arrive in Delhi?

Clerk:	It arrives at 4.30pm.
Tourist:	And which platform is the Delhi train on?
Clerk:	The Delhi train is on platform six.
(City)	... kii ek ticket kitne paise hay?

Replies:

(Bombay)	ek sao biis rupeya hay.
(Agra)	pachaas rupeya hay.
(Kanpur)	chaaliis rupeya hay.
(Jaipur)	biis rupeya hay.
(Jodpur)	tiis rupeya hay.
(Depart)	... kii gaaRi kab jaaegii?

Replies:

(Bombay)	... raat ko saava aaTH baje jaaegii.
(Agra)	... raat ko saaRHe gyaarah baje jaaegii.
(Kanpur)	... dinko das baje jaaegii.
(Jaipur)	... dinko nao baje jaaegii.
(Jodpur)	... dinko saava gyaarah baje jaaegii.
(Arrive)	aur kab ... pahuu#chegii?

Replies:

(Bombay)	raat ko saaRHe saat baje pahuu#chegii.
(Agra)	subah ko paa#ch baje pahuu#chegii.
(Kanpur)	dinko do baje pahuu#chegii.
(Jaipur)	dinko deRH baje pahuu#chegii.
(Jodpur)	dinko paune tiin baje pahuu#chegii.
(Platform)	aur ... kii gaaRii kis platform per hay?

Replies:

(Bombay)	... kii gaaRii do number platform per hay.
(Agra)	... kii gaaRii saat number platform per hay.
(Kanpur)	... kii gaaRii aaTH number platform per hay.
(Jaipur)	... kii gaaRii chaar number platform per hay.
(Jodpur)	... kii gaaRii ek number platform per hay.

Exercise 19

Sonya replies:
1a. mere tiin bhaaii hay.

2a. do buRe hay, aur ek chhoTa.
3a. meri ek behn hay.
4a. buRii.

Raja replies:
1a. mere do bhaaii hay.
2a. ek buRe hay, aur ek chhoTa.
3a. meri do behn hay.
4a. ek buRi hay, aur ek chhoTi.

Puja replies:
1a. mere tiin bhaaii hay.
2a. ek buRe hay, aur do chhoTa.
3a. meri ek behn hay.
4a. chhoTii.

Anil replies:
1a. mere do bhaaii hay.
2a. dono# chhoTe hay.
3a. meri do behn hay.
4a. dono# chhoTii hay.

Exercise 20

Ramesh replies:
a) ham Delhi me# rehte hay.
b) ham office me# kaam karte hay.
c) haa# jii, ham hindi jaante hay.
d) haa# jii, ham cigarette piite hay.
e) ek hazaar rupeya milte hay.
f) ham pachchiis saal ke hay.

Sonya replies:
a) ham Agra me# rehtii hay.
b) ham school me# kaam kartii hay.
c) haa# jii, ham bengali jaantii hay.
d) jii nahii#, ham cigarette nahii# piitii.
e) do hazaar rupeya milte hay.
f) ham tiis saal kii hay.

Sheila replies:
a) ham Bombay me# rehtii hay.
b) ham bank me# kaam kartii hay.
c) haa# jii, ham bengali jaantii hay.
d) jii nahii#, ham cigarette nahii# piitii.
e) tiin hazaar paa#ch sao rupeya milte hay.
f) ham biis saal kii hay.

Abdul replies:
a) ham Agra me# rehte hay.
b) ham factory me# kaam karte hay.
c) haa# jii, ham hindi jaante hay.
d) haa# jii, ham cigarette piite hay.
e) chaar hazaar saat sao rupeya milte hay.
f) ham chaaliis saal ke hay.

Exercise 21

a) ten minutes ago.	i) aaTH din ke baad.
b) three years ago.	j) ek mahiine hua.
c) after six months.	k) tiin saal hua.
d) one month ago.	l) das minute hua.
e) one year ago/before.	m) ek hafta ke baad.
f) after eight days.	n) chhe mahiine ke baad.
g) nine hours ago.	o) nao ghunTa hua.
h) after one week.	p) ek saal pehle.

Exercise 22

1. Bombay se – (a) Delhi (b) Madras (c) Calcutta – jaana, hawaaii-jahaaz se, kitne paise lagta hay?
1a. (a) do hazaar rupeya lagta hay; (b) saaRHe chaar hazaar rupeya lagta hay; (c) tiin hazaar rupeya lagta hay.

2. Bombay se – (a) Delhi (b) Madras (c) Calcutta – jaana, hawaii-jahaaz se, kitne ghunTa lagta hay?
2a. (a) tiin ghunTa lagta hay; (b) saaRHe chaar ghunTa lagta hay; (c) saaRHe tiin ghunta lagta hay.

3. Bombay se – *(a)* Delhi *(b)* Madras *(c)* Calcutta – jaana, bus se, kitne paise lagta hay?

3a. *(a)* do sao rupeya lagta hay; *(b)* saaRHe tiin sao rupeya lagta hay; *(c)* tiin sao rupeya lagta hay.

4. Bombay se – *(a)* Delhi *(b)* Madras *(c)* Calcutta – jaana, bus se, kitne ghunTa lagta hay?

4a. *(a)* das ghunTa lagta hay; *(b)* chaudah ghunTa lagta hay; *(c)* baara ghunTa lagta hay.

Exercise 23

Since this is primarily an oral exercise, and since you have a list of state capitals and languages to refer to, there is no need for a full set of answers. Simply repeat the question **kyo# ... aaye?**, *exchanging the city name each time, and reply by putting the appropriate language before the phrase* **siikhna ke liye**.

Exercise 24

Questions to Tara, and her replies:

a)	India kab aayii?	chaar hafte hua aayii.
b)	kab tak rehengii?	saaRHe tiin hafte rehengii.
c)	kahaa# gayii?	ham Delhi aur Bombay gayii.
d)	kyaa dekha?	Old Delhi dekha.
e)	Delhi me# kab se rehtii hay?	ham Delhi me# ek hafta se rehtii hay.
f)	Delhi me# kahaa# rehtii hay?	ham Hotel Vikram me# rehtii hay.
g)	kyo# India aayii?	ghuumna dekhna ke liye.

Questions to Sonya are the same as to Tara; Sonya replies:

a) nao hafte hua aayii.

b) tiin din rehengii.

c) ham Agra gayii.

d) Taj Mahal dekha.

e) ham Delhi me# chhe din se rehtii hay.

f) ham Gandhi Lodge me# rehtii hay.

g) kyo# nahii#?

Questions to Anil, and his replies:

a)	India kab aaye?	chhe din hua aaya.
b)	kab tak rehenge?	chaar mahiine rehenge.
c)	kahaa# gaye?	Varanaasi gaye.
d)	kyaa dekha?	Ganga Mai dekha.
e)	Delhi me# kab se rehte hay?	ham Delhi me# ek din se rehte hay.
f)	Delhi me# kahaa# rehte hay?	ham Gandhi Hotel me# rehte hay.
g)	kyo## India aaye?	sitar siikhna ke liye.

Exercise 25

1. Raja jii, aap India me# kahaa# jaaenge?
1a. ham Agra jaaenge.
2. aur Agra me# kab tak rehenge?
2a. ham ek hafta rehenge, phiir Bombay jaaenge.
3. aur Bombay me# kab tak rehenge?
3a. ham do hafta (tak) rehenge.

1. ... [Sonya/Sheila/Tara] jii, aap India me# kahaa# jaaengii?
1a. ham ... [Calcutta/Delhi/Jaipur] jaaengii.
2. aur ... [Calcutta/Delhi/Jaipur] me# kab tak rehengii?
2a. *Sonya:* ham das din rehengii, phiir Puri jaaengii.
   Sheila: ham do saal rehengii, phiir Agra jaaengii.
   Tara: ham paa#ch mahiine rehengii, phiir Madras jaaengii.

3. aur ... [Puri/Agra/Madras] me# kab tak rehengii?
3a. *Sonya:* ham chaar mahiine rehengii.
   Sheila: ham ek din rehengii.
   Tara: ham paa#ch saal rehengii.

Mini-dictionary

This is not a complete list of all vocabulary found in the book, but is a collection of words which you should find useful. The Hindi-English list is followed by an English-Hindi one, starting on page 138.

Hindi-English

aaj today
aa#kh eye
aafsos pity
aaluu potato
aanaa to come
aap you
aapkaa/ii/e your
aaTH eight
ab now
achchhaa/ii good
achchhaa! right! OK!
agar if
(ke) andar inside
angrezii English
apnaa my, your, his etc
arey! oh dear!
assii eighty
aTHaaraa eighteen
aur and

(ke) baad after (in time)
baa#h arm
(ke) baahar outside
baap father
baara twelve
baat thing
bachchaa child (boy), son

bachchii child (girl), daughter
bahut very, much
baiTHnaa to sit
banaanaa to make
baRaa/ii/e big, older
bas bus
bas enough
beTaa son
beTii daughter
bhaaii brother
bhii also
biibii wife
(ke) biich between
biis twenty
bolnaa to say, to speak
buraa bad

chaahnaa to want
chaaliis forty
chaar four
chaaval rice
chaay tea
chaudah fourteen
chhe six
chhoTaa/ii/e small, younger
daadaa grandfather (paternal)

daadii grandmother (paternal)
daal daal, lentils
dahii yoghurt
dard pain
das ten
das laakh one million
davaaii medicine
dekhnaa to see
denaa to give
din day
do two
dono# both
dopahar afternoon
draaiivar driver
dukaan shop
duudh milk

ek one
ek karoR ten million

farvarii February
fuTbaal football

gaanaa to sing, song
galaa throat
garam hot
garmii heat
ghanTaa hour
ghar house, home
ghii ghee, clarified butter
ghuumnaa-phirnaa walking, strolling
giTaar guitar
gobhi cauliflower
gosht meat
gundi dirty
gyaarah eleven
haa# yes
haal health

haftaa week
hay is
hay# are, is (polite)
ham we
hamaaraa our
havaaii jahaaz aeroplane
hazaar thousand
hii only
huu# am

inkaa his, her, their
is this, these, he, she etc
iskaa his, her, its

jaanaa to go
jab when
jahaa# where
jaisaa as
janvarii January
jii = mark of respect (sir/madam)
jii haa# yes
jii nahii# no
jis which
jitnaa as much
jo which

kaa of
kaafii much
kaam work
kaam karnaa to work
kaan ear
kaar car
kaarobaar business
kab? when?
kahaa# where
kaise how
kal tomorrow, yesterday
kam little, less
kamraa room
karnaa to do

135

kaun who
kaunsaa/ii/e? which?
khaaiiye please eat
khaanaa to eat
khaanaa food
kharaab bad
khonaa to lose
khiRkii window
kitaab book
kitnaa/ii/e how much,
   how many
ko to, at
koii any, some
kuchh some
kursii chair
kuttaa dog
kyaa what

laanaa to bring, to take
laakh hundred thousand
laRkaa boy
laRkii girl
lenaa take
lekin but
liijiye please take
likhnaa to write
(ke) liye for
log people

maa# mother
maataa mother
matar peas
magar but
may# I
masaalaa spice
mausam weather
me# in
meraa/ii/e my
mez table
milnaa to meet
mirch chilli

mujhe me, to me
mujhe afsos hay I am
   sorry

naak nose
naam name
naanaa grandfather
   (maternal)
naanii grandmother
   (maternal)
nabbe ninety
nahii# no, not
namak salt
namaste = Hindu greeting
nambar number
nao nine
(ke) niiche under, beneath

paa#ch five
paanii water
paao# foot
(ke) paas near
pachaas fifty
pachchiis twenty-five
(se) pahle before (in time)
paise money
pakaanaa to cook
par on, at
paRhnaa to read
paRhaanaa to teach
pataa address
pati husband
patnii wife
pehle first
peT stomach
phir again, then
phuul flower
piinaa to drink, smoke
(ke) piichhe behind
pitaa husband
pleT plate

pondrah fifteen

raastaa road
raat night
rakhnaa to keep
rehnaa to live, to stay
rupeyaa rupee

saal year
(ke) saamne in front of
saat seven
saaTH sixty
(ke) saath with
sab all
sabzii vegetable
safar journey
sangiit music
sao hundred
sar-dard headache
sardii cold
satrah seventeen
sattar seventy
se from, by
shaadii married
shaam evening
shuruu beginning
siikhnaa to learn
sir head
solah sixteen
subah morning

sunnaa to listen, to hear

tab then
tairnaa to swim
takliif difficulty
tandoor oven
terah thirteen
THiik fine, OK
thoRaa a little
tiin three
tiis thirty
tum you (fam.)
tumhaaraa your
Tuu#Tnaa to break
tuu you (very fam.)

u#glii finger
unkaa their
unniis nineteen
us him, her
uskaa his, her
(ke) uupar on, above
vahaa# there
ve he, she, they etc
voh he, she, it

yaa or
yahaa# here
ye they, this etc
yeh he, she, it, etc

English-Hindi

address **pataa**
above **(ke) uupar**
aeroplane **havaaii jahaaz**
after (in time) **(ke) baad**
afternoon **dopahar**
again **phir**
all **sab**
also **bhii**
am **huu#**
and **aur**
any **koii**
are, is (polite) **hay#**
arm **baa#h**
as **jaisaa**
as much **jitnaa**
at **par, ko**

bad **buraa, kharaab**
before (in time) **(se) pahle**
beginning **shuruu**
behind **(ke) piichhe**
beneath **(ke) niiche**
between **(ke) biich**
big **baRaa/ii/e**
book **kitaab**
both **dono#**
boy **laRkaa**
break (v.) **Tu#Tnaa**
bring (v.) **laanaa**
brother **bhaaii**
bus **bas**
business **kaarobaar**
but **lekin, magar**
by **se**

call (v.) **kehnaa**
car **kaar**
cauliflower **gobhi**
chair **kursii**

child (boy) **bachchaa**
child (girl) **bachchii**
cold **sardii**
come, to **aanaa**
cook (v.) **pakaanaa**

daughter **beTii**
day **din**
difficulty **taKliff**
dirty **gundi**
do (v.) **karnaa**
dog **kuttaa**
drink (v.) **piinaa**
driver **draaiivar**

ear **kaan**
eat (v.) **khaanaa**
eight **aaTH**
eighteen **aTHaaraa**
eighty **assii**
eleven **gyaarah**
English **angrezii**
enough **bas**
evening **shaam**
eye **aa#kh**

father **baap**
fifteen **pondrah**
fifty **pachaas**
fine **THiik**
finger **u#glii**
first **pehle**
five **paa#ch**
flower **phuul**
food **khaanaa**
foot **paao#**
football **fuTbaal**
for **(ke) liye**
forty **chaaliis**

four **chaar**
fourteen **chaudah**
from **se**
in front of **(ke) saamne**

ghee **ghii**
girl **laRkii**
give (v.) **denaa**
go (v.) **jaanaa**
good **achchhaa/ii**
grandfather
   (paternal) **daadaa**
   (maternal) **naanaa**
grandmother
   (paternal) **daadii**
   (maternal) **naanii**
guitar **giTaar**

he **is, ve, voh**
head **sir**
headache **sar-dard**
health **haal**
hear (v.) **sunaa**
heat **garmii**
hello **namaste** (Hindu
   greeting)
her **inkaa, iskaa, us, uskaa**
here **yahaa#**
him **us**
his **inkaa, iskaa, uskaa,**
   apnaa
hot **garam**
hour **ghanTaa**
house, home **ghar**
how **kaisaa, kaise**
how much, how many
   kitnaa/ii/e
hundred **sao**
husband **pati, pitaa**

I **may#**

if **agar**
in **me#**
inside **(ke) andar**
is **hay**
it **voh, yeh**

journey **safar**

learn (v.) **siikhnaa**
lentils **daal**
less **kam**
listen (v.) **sunnaa**
little **kam**
   a little **thoRaa**
live (v.) **rehnaa**

make (v.) **banaanaa**
married **shaadii**
me, to me **mujhe**
meat **gosht**
medicine **davaaii**
meet (v.) **milnaa**
milk **duudh**
money **paise**
morning **subah**
mother **maa#, maataa**
much **bahut, kaafii**
music **sangiit**
my **meraa/ii/e, apnaa**

name **naam**
near **(ke) paas**
needed
   is needed **chaahiiye**
   are needed **chaahiiye#**
night **raat**
nine **nao**
nineteen **unniis**
ninety **nabbe**
no, not **nahii#, jii nahii#**
nose **naak**

now **ab**
number **nambar**

of **kaa**
oh dear! **arey!**
OK **THiik**
on **par**
one **ek**
only **hii**
or **yaa, ki**
our **hamaaraa**
outside **(ke) baahar**
oven **tandoor**

pain **dard**
peas **matar**
people **log**
pity **aafsos**
place **rakh**
plate **pleT**
potato **aaluu**

read (v.) **paRhnaa**
rice **chaaval**
right! **achchhaa!**
road **raastaa**
rupee **rupeyaa**

salt **namak**
say (v.) **bolnaa**
see (v.) **dekhnaa**
seven **saat**
seventeen **satrah**
seventy **sattar**
she **is, ve, voh, yeh**
shop **dukaan**
sing (v.) **gaanaa**
sister **bahan**
sit (v.) **baiTHnaa**
six **chhe**
sixteen **solah**

sixty **saaTH**
small **chhoTaa/ii/e**
smoke (v.) **piinaa**
some **koii, kuchh**
son **bachchaa, beTaa**
song **gaanaa**
sorry, I am **mujhe afsos
    hay**
speak (v.) **bolnaa**
spice **masaalaa**
stay (v.) **rehnaa**
stomach **peT**
swim (v.) **tair**

table **mez**
take (v.) **lenaa**
    take **lo**
    please take **liijiye**
tea **chaay**
teach (v.) **paRhaanaa,
    sikhaanaa**
ten **das**
their **inkaa, unkaa**
then **phir, tab**
there **vahaa#**
they **ve, ye**
thing **baat**
this, these **is**
thirteen **terah**
thirty **tiis**
this **ye**
thousand **hazaar**
three **tiin**
throat **galaa**
to **ko**
today **aaj**
tomorrow **kal**
twelve **baara**
twenty **biis**
twenty-five **pachchiis**
two **do**

vegetable **sabzii**
very **bahut**

walking **ghuumnaa-phirnaa**
want (v.) **chaahnaa**
water **paanii**
we **ham**
weather **mausam**
week **haftaa**
what **kyaa**
when **jab**
    when? **kab?**
where **jahaa#**
which **jo, jis**
    which? **kaunsaa/ii/e?**
who **kaun**

wife **biibii, patnii**
window **khiRkii**
with **(ke) saath**
work **kaam**
    work (v.) **kaam karnaa**
write (v.) **likhnaa**

year **saal**
yes **haa#, jii haa#**
yesterday **kal**
yoghurt **dahii**
you **aap**
    (fam.) **tum**
    (very fam.) **tuu**
younger **chhoTaa/ii/e**
your **aapkaa/ii/e, apnaa, tumhaaraa**

Index

Picture Credits